The First Adman

Thomas Bish and the Birth of Modern Advertising

by Gary Hicks

Published by

Victorian Secrets Limited
32 Hanover Terrace
Brighton BN2 9SN

www.victoriansecrets.co.uk

The First Adman: Thomas Bish and the Birth of Modern Advertising
by Gary Hicks

A catalogue record for this book is available from the British Library.

ISBN 978-1-906469-39-9

CONTENTS

PREFACE

Admen, if asked to name the original 'giants' of their trade, will usually cite the American tycoons Albert Davis Lasker (Pepsodent, Kleenex, Palmolive) and Leo Burnett (Marlboro Man, the Green Giant). Another is likely to be the visionary Marcel Bleustein-Blanchet, pioneer of radio commercials and founder of France's first advertising agency Publicis. There is David Ogilvy, who brought British style to American advertising after World War Two, and Bill Bernach, who led a creative revolution in the 1940s and 1950s by mixing words and visuals (Polaroid film, Levi's Jeans) and later pioneered the idea of ironical ads (Volkswagen). An acclaimed modern innovator is John Hegarty who gave German car maker Audi its legendary strapline *Vorsprung durch Technik* and founded Bartle, Bogle and Hegarty, one of the world's most famous ad agencies.

Yet few of the millions working for the industry worldwide will be aware that their bright new ideas for selling products have all been tried before – not by these celebrated pioneers but more than two centuries ago by the first celebrity admen, Bish and Son, to promote the British state lottery.

The lucky draw then was as effective as it is now in raising money for good causes; more than £2 billion in today's money in the thirty years to 1826, when Parliament abolished the lottery. Tickets were sold through the promotional genius of stockjobber Thomas Bish and his even more talented son, also called Thomas Bish, earning them both a vast fortune and making them early media stars more famous than successive Prime Ministers. In doing so, father and son, their brand as famous in its day as Coca-Cola is now, practically invented advertising and marketeering.

Among the many techniques the Bishes pioneered were integrated promotional campaigns, 'spin doctoring', graphic design, visual tricks in posters and handbills, original typography, direct mail, direct marketing and even market research.

Now they have been airbrushed out of history, without so much as an entry in *The Oxford Dictionary of National Biography*. Their name is forgotten, but their legacy survives all around us in all media. This is the story of the true begetters of advertising. Their resurrection is long overdue.

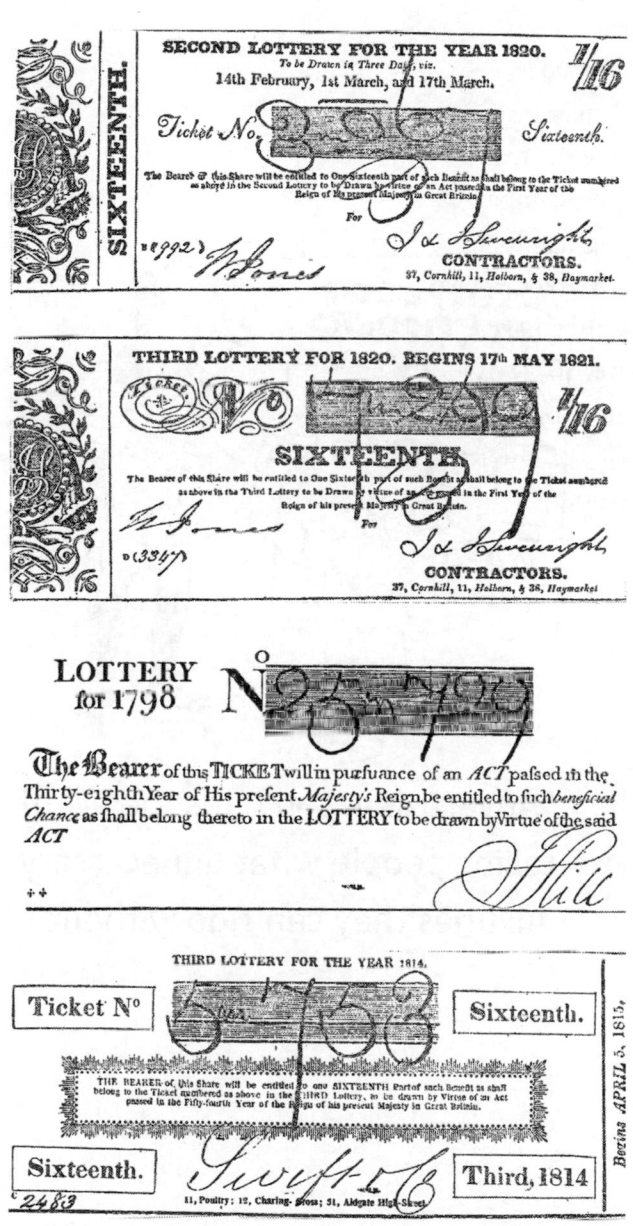

State lottery tickets

"Advertising, son? It's the art of telling people what unnecessary luxuries they can't do without"

CHAPTER ONE

A Shaky Start

Coxheath Camp, Kent, September 1778

As Britain braced itself for the expected French invasion, the atmosphere became febrile. Only six months earlier France had joined the American rebels in their increasingly successful two-year-old War of Independence against the British, opening up a new front in Europe. Now, French and Spanish warships dominated the Channel, increasing insecurity. Britain's forces of just 50,000 men, 28,000 of them mainly untrained militia, fell 'very short of what is reckoned necessary for the defence of England alone,' warned the *London Chronicle*. And their arms and supplies, provided by corrupt Government contractors, remained notoriously sub-standard despite regular public outcries about 'harpy Agents grinding the faces of their species'.

Well might baritone Mr. Lowe, a kind of male Vera Lynn of the time, seek to lift morale with spirited patriotic songs belted out during the interval at Sadler's Wells musical productions. Audiences wildly applauded the rather McGonagallish chorus:

For should the Monsieurs dare to land on our shore
We quickly would make them for quarter to roar
And beg pardon and promise to do so no more.

But the reality was that the country, as it would 162 years later during other nervous September days, stood alone against the world, and its defences were inadequate to the task.

As in 1940, the Battle of Britain was thought certain to take place in Kent. To protect London from the threatened advance of the monsieurs, a vast military camp of 15,000 men, three miles long, seven miles in circumference, was built on an empty heath two miles south of Maidstone. Regular regiments and volunteers from Cornwall to Yorkshire were stationed in this tented city, which soon attracted so many sightseers and hangers-on, women especially, that a London-Coxheath coach service was started (seven shillings, half price outside, and luggage at a halfpenny per pound for the seven-hour journey).

'It is impossible to stop laughing at the prodigious number of women of all sorts and sizes and of all ages who flock from all parts to see the camp,' wrote one subaltern to a friend. Typical of the many female domestic servants who played truant from work to visit this fashionable destination was Amy Lyon, a young feisty chambermaid employed by Mr. Budd, a surgeon at St. Bartholomew's Hospital in London. On return to her duties, she was instantly dismissed but later won fame and fortune as Lord Nelson's Emma Hamilton. At the other end of the social spectrum Georgiana, Duchess of Devonshire, led a gang of aristocratic groupies nicknamed 'the beauteous Amazons' who rode around in low phaetons drawn by ponies during morning exercises, cheering up the men and showing off their fetching military-style riding attire and jaunty cockades. Local women, both low prostitutes and respectable matrons with an eye to the main chance, invaded in loaded caravans. 'Bedawbed' courtesans from Covent Garden arrived in one-horse gigs 'stowed together as close as bale goods for an East India voyage'. Middle-class adventuresses claimed loose acquaintanceship with young officers in order to gatecrash the glittering, candle-lit soirees held nightly in the rows of marquees to the sound of hautboys, clarinets, and kettle-drums.

Virtually everyone was on the make. The spivs who supplied

two waggons of bread daily from specially built giant ovens at Mr. Shephard's Wharf in Maidstone had so adulterated the product that it was commonly regarded as not even fit to give to hogs. Profiteering was rife. The Star Inn charged a scandalous one shilling per head for 'very indifferent tea, coarse sugar and common milk,' compared to eight pence at the public booths. Landlords cashed in, extorting exorbitant rents for houses in adjacent villages used as field hospitals and for mansions used as living quarters by wealthy officers tired of life under canvass. Farmers exploited the naïve provincial militiamen. 'I gave seven shillings for two fowls no bigger than blackbirds and half a crown for a pint of peas,' complained one in his diary. At the same time the crafty Kentish rustics, playing shrewdly on the boredom induced by waiting for the fight with the French, used the military to help gather the hops early in that exceptionally hot summer. They got their comeuppance later, however, when some soldiers began stealing chickens, sheep and also geese, roasting some and using others for sentry duty, as they famously did in Ancient Rome.

Among the many chancers intent on milking the Coxheath cash cow was a budding entrepreneur who was quicker than most to seize the commercial opportunities of the encampment. He was an obscure stationer from the burgeoning Piccadilly district of the capital, who gave up his business there to seek his fortune amid the preparations for war. One of the first acts of this promotional genius was to set up shop by the stop where the London coach disgorged its passengers. Newspaper notices advertising the thrice weekly service helpfully mentioned this fact. 'Fly continues going … at Seven to MR. BISH's Stationer, nearly opposite the center of the Camp.' It was a modest start for Thomas Bish who, helped by his son also called Thomas, was to become a national figure known everywhere as 'Lucky Bish' as he revolutionised advertising and promotion.

Twenty years earlier Dr. Johnson wrote, 'The trade of advertising is now so near to perfection that it is not easy to propose any improvement.' For once, the great man was wrong. Newspaper advertisements then differed little in style from the first known one published in the weekly news book, *Mercurius Britannicus* in February 1625. It promised:

> Here is this present day published an excellent discourse concerning the match between our most Gracious and Mightie Prince Charles, Prince of Wales and the Lady Henrietta Marie daughter to Henry the Fourth, late King of France. ... With the lively picture of the Prince and Lady cut in Brasse.

For about 150 years advertisements followed this pattern. They were mainly simple announcements for books, plays, prints, lotteries, wines, teas, patent medicines, luxury items, wax candles, pickles, turtles, hair oil, locks, furniture, millinery, shipping movements, auctions and oddities, such as viper wines to cure impotence. Few would have passed the present-day Advertising Standards Commission 'truthful, fair and honest' test. Life pills 'discovered by the Rev. C. Carrington, Vicar of Berkeley and Deputy Lieutenant of Gloucestershire' promised to cure everything, even cancer of the bowel. Mr. Piper of 238 High Street, Exeter, announced his intention of killing a specially fattened Russian bear for its grease 'to make hair grow on heads that were absolutely bald'. Locks were claimed to be unbreakable: 'one hundred guineas reward to any locksmith who can unpick them'.

But as the industrial revolution gathered pace, creating a nascent consumer society and celebrity culture, sophistication grew and brand names were established and marketed. Mass-produced fans, snuff boxes, playing cards, porcelain figures and ceramic tiles decorated with portraits of famous actresses sold in their thousands. One of the first to advertise systematically in newspapers was the potter Josiah Wedgwood, who also pioneered marketing innovations such as inertia selling (sending unsolicited goods) and travelling salesmen. He was followed by Robert Warren, manufacturer of 'original matchless' boot polish, Alexander Rowland, purveyor of celebrated Macassar Oil for the hair, Samuel Solomon, quack doctor and inventor of the

Cordial Balm of Gilead, who spent £5,000 a year on ads, and George Packwood, inventor of razor strops and proprietary paste. In 1795, George sold 10,000 of his products through a single outlet, using sixty separate ads in nearly thirty different newspapers with such immortal lines as:

> In the compting-house the smart City blade,
> Before he is dressed for the shop
> The razor can flourish, what gives him the aid?
> Why Packwood's ingenious Strop

Even bear's grease moved from the freak show era, when the animals were sometimes kept in barbers' shops as sales gimmicks, into the mainstream in the form of an animal fat-based hair dressing manufactured by James Atkinson.

What distinguished the Bishes from the rest of these self-publicists was their strategy of integrating newspapers, journals, direct mail, posters, handbills, street processions, promotional carts, imaginative graphics and spin doctoring into cleverly targeted nationwide marketing operations. Father, then son, used writers, illustrators and advertising agents in a fresh and imaginative way to create a brand by systematic, regular and persistent use of all media then available. For nearly forty years the Bish name was repeated constantly in newspaper advertisements, establishing a format that has been copied constantly through a kind of collective folk memory of every successful brand ever since.

For the ambitious twenty-seven-year-old Thomas, networking hard at Coxheath, all this was for the future. No likeness of him survives, save for a sketch with the punning title *The City Chance-Seller* (of lottery tickets) dated 1815, the year of his death. It shows a tall, ruggedly handsome man, dressed in fashionable top hat and greatcoat. The confident, slightly arrogant, expression suggests he would have found no difficulty in crossing the class divide. Its rigidity is glimpsed in the newspaper column *Camp Intelligence* syndicated on 3 September; reports of deserting privates and corporals punished with 1,000 lashes of the cat-o'-nine-tails (virtually a death sentence) sit oddly with details of elegant regimental balls and suppers given by officers for their ladies and 'most of the Nobility on the Heath.' Bish was a cheerful and sociable guest at these events, where he exploited his position as main supplier of the reams of stationery, books and other materials required in order to cultivate useful contacts. Lieutenant General William Keppel, Commander-in-Chief of the encamped forces, commissioned him to produce and supply a map of the complex camp for use by both militia and the regular regiments stationed there, as required by Act of Parliament. Measuring twenty-four by fourteen inches, this beautifully coloured and accurate little aid for finding the way round the miles of tents on the sprawling heath, clearly shows the disposition of forces, their strengths and their facings. In its simplicity and linear graphic design, it is not unlike Harry Beck's groundbreaking London underground map of the 1930s, or the classic standardized road signage systems developed by Margaret Calvert and Jock Kinneir in 1964 still used today. There is a copy in the British Library and at least three others in various county archives, which suggests it was a treasured souvenir handed down through the generations. Although the detail was almost certainly measured and drawn by a numerate soldier, it has the stamp of Bish's nascent communications skills all over it, skills he was to exploit brilliantly when James Branscomb, stockjobber, City dignitary and twenty years his senior, took him under his wing as a junior business partner.

At that time it was common for stockjobbers, who dealt with stocks and shares on behalf of brokers, to run the state lottery which had been around since 1694. Not only did it raise money for continuing government spending, like feeding the navy, but it also funded specific projects from providing London's first clean drinking water to founding the British Museum. Everyone played it, from the daughters of King George III to poor female domestic servants. Poor people often won, though as now their sudden unexpected wealth did not always guarantee happiness. Mr. Alder, who made a meagre living as a cooper and publican, won £20,000 in a 1767 draw, a huge sum then (more than £1 million in today's money). He gave most of it away to neighbours and local charities in the Berkshire town of Abingdon (now part of Oxfordshire) where he lived, but was so pressurised by greedy supplicants demanding money that the good-hearted man suffered a nervous breakdown. The draws, held over forty days before excited crowds at London's Guildhall, were pure theatre. Two huge rotating drums six feet in diameter (one containing ticket counterfoils, the other prize tickets and blanks) were spun faster and faster until finally stopped for two Bluecoat boys from Christ's Hospital to pull out, simultaneously, a ticket number and its fate. Dramatically, amid cheers or boos, a clerk yelled out the result, which could be a cash prize worth up to £3 million today. The *Morning Chronicle* of 28 January 1794 listed lucky winners as 'Mr. Taylor the Hatter on Tower Hill, a £20,000 prize. Also £10,000 by Mr. Hackelton of the Borough. They are both retired from business. £20,000 to a merchant in Ireland, £10,000 to a gentleman who frequents the Bank, £5,000 to Thomas Johnes MP for Radnor, and £5,000 to Miss Edmonds near Epsom, Surrey.' Among more famous winners was the novelist and dramatist Mary Russell Mitford, who won £20,000 with a ticket her father bought her as a present on her tenth birthday. She squandered it all, as have so many big winners since.

Arrangements for organising the game were bureaucratic and cumbersome, but the principle was the same as in the UK National Lottery today; the government awarded the license to the contractor it believed would raise the most money for the public purse. The difference was that, whereas now a license runs for seven years, as does Camelot's from February 2009, then it was for a few months only to cover each individual lottery. The procedure was that the Chancellor of the Exchequer annually announced details of the prizes, number of tickets and dates of the two or three State lotteries to be

held during the year and invited bids to run it. The bidders, mainly
stockjobbers, submitted in sealed envelopes their offer price per ticket.
The highest offer won the contract, although there were usually hours
of acrimonious wrangling over details as Ministers, desperate for cash
to fight the French, squeezed the maximum amount possible for their
coffers. On at least one occasion they threatened to nationalise the
game and run it themselves if the contractors did not offer enough.
Sometimes, consortiums were formed. In 1799, the bidders who met
William Pitt at Number Ten Downing Street with their proposals
were Bish, Branscomb, Richardson, Cooper, Beardmore, £13.10s.
6d; Hazard, Capel, Stephenson £13. 15s. 4d; Cope, Curtis, Goldsmid,
Salomon £14. 0s. 5d; and Shewell, Towgood, Ellis, Grenville £14. 1s.
5d, who won. Tickets may seem expensive at this price, but each was
usually split into sixteen shares which allowed low-paid workers such
as servants and office clerks the chance to club together to purchase
a stake.

The real winners were the lottery operators, whose average annual
salary was £10,000 (£300,000 today). So it was scarcely surprising that
once the invasion scare subsided and the camp scaled down, Bish
opted for a smart career move and joined dozens of other hopefuls in
the lottery business. He almost certainly met his mentor Branscomb
during the endless social whirl that was Coxheath, as it was fashionable
for City men to do their patriotic duty and visit the troops. The two
set up three offices in London at No. 187 Fleet Street, No. 4 Cornhill
and No. 11 Holborn. They were increasingly successful in winning
contracts to run both the English and Irish lotteries, making regular
trips to Dublin and successfully lobbying for a fast coach service to
whisk draw results from there to London via a wherry. They also ran
the occasional tontine, a bizarre life insurance gamble, invented by
Neapolitan banker Lorenzo Tonti, where the shares to a loan increase
in value as subscribers die off until the last survivor inherits everything.

Competition was intense since the Grafton Government changed
the rules a decade earlier to allow huge cash sums to be paid out as

prizes. It was also testosterone-fuelled; out of thirty-six entrepreneurs listed in 1796 as being authorised to run lotteries only one was a woman, Sarah Shower of No. 71 New Bond Street. All were skilled in publicity. One found an old woman in the country called Goodluck and paid her £50 a year to use her name. Pope located his business on the Royal Exchange close to the Bank of England, branded it 'The Fortunate Lottery Office' and won a good market share. William Nicholson, then the dominant lottery broker, regularly published the names of lucky winners such as 'Nathaniel Crozer, a Smithfield Shoemaker', and 'Joseph Welsh, Organist of Newbury, Berks', an obvious marketing ploy which inexplicably Bish never used, boasting it was his 'invariable rule'. His explanation that naming winners 'might be unpleasant' does not ring true. So he simply described the recipient of the largest prize ever won in the old State lottery, £50,000 (£2.5 million today), as 'a Gentleman from Hampshire'.

Bish, tempted by money to indulge his wide boy side, did not make an auspicious start. In addition to the official draw there were complex schemes called 'insurances' which allowed the poor to bet a shilling on a specific number coming up on a specific day, and winning a pound if it did. Betting on numbers in this way was as illegal then as it is today. Yet Bish, even after he became a licensed lottery house keeper in 1790, took these side bets in parallel to the legitimate business he ran with Branscomb. For years he got away with it but, eventually, he was found out, prosecuted on the evidence of a client Duggan McCarty, found guilty on three charges and fined £50 on each charge. For Bish, a churchwarden for the parish of St. Mary Woolchurch Haw, as well as for the even more respectable Branscomb, philanthropist, governor of St. Bartholomew's Hospital and future lay sheriff of London, this was deeply embarrassing. Yet he compounded the offence by not paying up and, as a result, on 12 December 1793 was brought to court before Lord Chief Justice Kenyon at the Guildhall where the jury, after a long debate, convicted him of non-payment.

With extraordinary foolishness, Bish continued issuing insurances, only to fall into the clutches of an unpleasant extortioner, Robert Jacques, who acted with a crooked lawyer called Wilkinson. Blackmailing lottery men in the late eighteenth century was common sport. One sharp crook, realising the chance of winning a prize was much less than advertised, threatened to expose the true value of the tickets. Late one Saturday night he placarded London with huge posters so that churchgoers could see them on Sunday. The posters displayed full-sized drawings of Bluecoat boys. The caption read, 'Unless the young gentlemen are very active, they will not have sufficient time to draw the thousands of blanks out of the wheel.' Ticket sales fell dramatically, causing the draw to be delayed three times. Eventually, the lottery operators bought off the extortioner with a hefty life pension.

In Jacques's scam, lottery office keepers were targeted according to their income and repeatedly forced to pay up on a sliding scale for each offence (£50 for rich William Nicholson down to £10 for a Mr. Newton) or face exposure and a possible £500 fine and three months' imprisonment. For a surprisingly long time Bish paid the Danegeld at £30 and £40 a time before coming to his senses and taking a stand not only for himself but also for his colleagues, who were increasingly seeing him as their spokesman. He collected as many of the blackmail letters as were available and produced them at the King's Bench Court where Jacques was tried on 11 July 1794. For the defence serjeant Kirby, complaining bitterly about being given only ten minutes' notice of his brief, attacked Bish's credibility as a witness, contending, 'He is not worthy of credit, both on account of the illegal nature of his business, as dealing in insurances, and his having so repeatedly compromised where he should have pursued at law.' Kenyon, however, directed that his testimony was 'just and satisfactory' and the jury, without hesitation, found Jacques guilty of perjury.

Three years later Bish again appeared before Kenyon, this time in a civil case involving a dispute over a forged £25 Bill of Exchange which he had accepted in payment for some lottery tickets. The *Morning Chronicle* reported, 'he brought his books with him into Court, by which it appeared his business was so extensive that he paid £9000 into his banker's hands on the very day when this transaction happened.' Kenyon, despite being notoriously anti-gambling, seemed to have liked the lottery keeper, as he commented, 'How was it possible for a man in great trade to know the precise pedigree of every Bill that came into his hands? If the law was otherwise, there would be an end of the great Paper credit of this country.' He said no fraud could be attributed to Bish, who won the case and was awarded damages, an important outcome that helped the 1797 campaign by bankers and merchants to get the newfangled banknotes more widely accepted.

That same year Thomas Bish, assisted by his teenaged son, felt confident enough to go it alone, taking over Branscomb's office at No. 4 Cornhill, expanding into No. 9 Charing Cross in 1801 and setting up permanent offices in Manchester and Edinburgh. Soon they had branches or agents in every main town in Britain and Ireland. There were goldsmiths in Norwich, silversmiths in Bradford, printers in Chester, hatters in Maidstone, booksellers in Aberdeen and Inverness, druggists in Tunbridge, chemists in Axbridge, perfumers in Woodbridge, the Post Office in Ilminster, and the Waggon Office in Monmouth … all doing a roaring trade in selling tickets, despite the known hazard that parcels of tickets were sometimes stolen from the mail coaches on their long journeys to London.

As well as developing a sophisticated retail chain, the consummate spin doctor began developing the marketing initiatives which were to make him the dominant lottery broker. Lottery puffs began appearing in news columns. In the *True Briton* of 13 July 1797, a psychologically clever paragraph warning that buyers should hurry to buy tickets in the Irish lottery as prices 'are sure to rise' appears among items about an unfortunate soap-boiler called Tansley who fell into one of his copper vessels and was scalded to death 'on the spot', a complaint by the Committee of Wine Merchants to William Pitt on a £300,000 deficiency in wine duties, a pantomime review and crime reports. At the same time Bish was winning blanket media coverage of prizewinning tickets he had sold; news of a £20,000 win in the March 1798 draw appeared in the *Sun*, *The Times*, *Morning Post*, *Star*, *St. James's Chronicle*, *Morning Herald*, *Oracle and Public Advertiser*, *True Briton*, and the *Observer*. And the ads themselves began snappier with claims such as 'Sixty Thousand Pounds may be gained by a single ticket' and 'a thousand winning tickets in one draw' grabbing the reader's attention. Novelties were introduced; players were offered any numbers they fancied, there were prizes for first drawn tickets and prizes for tickets drawn ending in a particular numeral.

Typographical innovation played its part, too. Bish hijacked the eye-catching loud and bold 'fat-faced' typefaces, which the pioneering London type designer Robert Thorne had developed for posters, using them as early as 1810 in handbills and newspaper advertisements. Although the parliamentary printer, Thomas Hansard, later denounced these early display faces as 'typographical monstrosities', they quickly caught on; Drury Lane Theatre used them in playbills, the publishers of 'penny dreadfuls' liked the exaggerated letters, and the bookseller and campaigning journalist William Hone deployed them to dramatic effect in the infamous political satires which landed him in prison. Another early convert, using them most imaginatively in his catalogues, was the flamboyant cockney auctioneer George Robins, whom Dickens lampooned. They have since been widely featured in print promotions and can be seen today in every newspaper or magazine, advertising virtually everything from Ryanair flights to banking services.

Bish could not, by himself, have succeeded in pushing through these new ideas; he needed what marketers now call 'a strategic partner', and found one in a tall, good-looking printer from Bristol called Frederick Gye. 'I know of a gentleman who amassed a considerable fortune (so as to be able to keep his carriage) by printing nothing but lottery placards and handbills of a colossal size,' wrote the essayist William Hazlitt. He almost certainly meant Gye, whose entrepreneurial spirit led him later into many business ventures with Bish's son, including selling tea and wine and running the famous London pleasure ground of Vauxhall Gardens. Both were also to become controversial Members of Parliament. On the eve before one draw, Bish (who was by then running his father's business) gave him a batch of unsold lottery tickets and Gye, rather suspiciously, won a prize of £30,000.

In 1806, however, Gye was just another jobbing printer working with a G. Balne from offices off Broad Street in the City of London, winning some government contracts for printing state lottery tickets and posters, with Carter's Directory listing all prizewinning numbers drawn in London. The introduction of the controversial typefaces that year marked the start of a creative partnership between Bish and Gye which encompassed not only other visual innovations, mainly in handbills as newspaper advertisements had yet to carry illustrations, but also improved copywriting. As the specialist divisions of today's advertising agencies, split into designers, copywriters, account handlers, and art directors did not exist, ideas flowed from all kinds of unlikely sources. The publisher Henry Vizetelly recalls in his memoirs, written in extreme old age in 1893, how his father James, a printer with an original mind, was one of them. 'He gave Gye some clever ideas for lottery posters which took Bish's fancies and led to extensive printing,' he wrote. In return Gye gave his father, who worked with Robert Branston, a famous wood engraver, 'a present of several hundreds of pounds.' That was how the system worked.

Bish Senior also became involved in other money-making schemes. The French Revolution had swept away the securities markets of Amsterdam and Paris, boosting London whose sharp dealers were quick to step into the breach. They set up the London Stock Exchange, which formally came into being as the first regulated exchange in March 1801, taking over from the loose securities markets that had existed before. Within months it moved from the old chaotic dealing room under a coffee shop in Sweeting's Alley to a new building in Capel Court in the heart of the City. The lottery entrepreneur became one of its first members. In the early days, the stockjobbers were a rough crowd much amused by violently bashing top hats down over people's mouths and then rolling them round the dealing room. Just after Christmas 1805 a man called Daws, clerk to the broker William Haynes was expelled 'for injuring Joseph Munyard's coat by vitriol'. Six weeks later Bish himself was physically harassed by two fellow brokers, the brothers William and Charles Thompson, who prevented him from working. He complained to the Exchange committee who let them off with a reprimand and a warning 'to preserve peace and order'. They were also however capable, under Bish's tutelage, of sophisticated press management. In its first year of existence the Exchange set up an enquiry into the 1801 lottery which, it was felt, had been manipulated by some members (not Bish). Its proceedings were leaked in an unhelpful manner to the *Oracle*, a morning newspaper unsympathetic to the fledgling Exchange. Immediately a letter was drafted and sent to the other editors who all printed it the following day. The template, which still survives in the Stock Exchange archives, reads, 'To the Editor of …. In Consequence of a partial misrepresented Statement of the Report of the Stock Exchange Committee having appeared in one of the morning papers (*Oracle*, 8 December 1801) of this day, the Committee feel it incumbent on them to request that you will not copy the same into your paper as they conceive it to have been inserted for malicious purposes.' No modern 'rebuttal unit' could have done better.

Early in the new century Bish had every reason to feel quietly confident, both personally and professionally. He had deflected, through political contacts, a potential knock-out blow by the reformer William Cobbett that the government should nationalise the lucky draw and run it at a fraction of the cost; his son Thomas had made a good match, marrying Mary, second daughter of John Collier from Newport, Shropshire, in August 1800; their bold move in breaking away from Branscomb was paying off in lucrative government contracts, the stock-jobbing business was prospering, their willingness to innovate meant they were beginning to pull away from the competition; and, most crucially, he was determined to stay on the right side of the law. For the next few years not only did he pioneer the marketing and advertising techniques we rely on today but he played a major role in resolving some of the most sensational financial scandals ever to hit the City of London.

"In those days, bankers used to get it in the neck – literally"

CHAPTER TWO

Scandals

Bish had become public-spirited, but only up to a point. Where duty clashed with business, business always won. That was why in 1806 he refused, on the grounds of lacking the time, to serve as sheriff for London and Middlesex, characteristically omitting to pay the customary fine of £400 for not fulfilling the legal duties involved and was obliged to make a compromise offer of £600 to the Court of Common Council (the City's parliament) to be excused. Luckily for him, the offer was accepted. He never seemed to be out of the courts. Once, he sued the fashionable Parisian dentist Nicholas Dubois de Chemant, who had fled to London to escape the revolutionary terror, and set up a lucrative business manufacturing porcelain dentures shaped from porcelain paste supplied by Josiah Wedgwood's company. He made 12,000 of them for the British and European market and, with Bish acting as his stockjobber, used the profits to speculate on the stock market. The two fell out over an outstanding sum of £2,200 the litigious lottery man claimed he was owed from a complicated share deal. The row was celebrated in *Real Life in London* which said Bish 'proved a hard-mouthed customer to the man of teeth and was not a quiet subject to be drawn but brought an action against the mineral monger and recovered the debt'. He gave evidence against

James 'Putty' Parsey, a glazier's apprentice who burgled his home at
No. 4 Cornhill and was sentenced to death, and he frequently appeared
at the Old Bailey as an expert witness in cases of stolen or forged
banknotes. On one occasion William Andrews, a Post Office sorter,
was sentenced to death at the Old Bailey for stealing a letter containing
£180 in banknotes on evidence from Bish from whom he had bought
lottery ticket Number 1257 with one of the notes.

A much more significant scalp, which shot Bish to national
attention, was that of Robert Astlett, the most senior and most
trusted cashier at the Bank of England, who had conned the bank
of £200,000. Bish uncovered this fraud when Astlett asked him, in
his role as purchaser of government securities, to dispose of three
Exchequer Bills worth £1,000 each. Sharp as ever, he quickly realised
they had already passed through his hands and had been deposited with
the bank, and so were clearly forged. He instantly alerted the Deputy
Governor, Mr. Winthrope, who had Astlett arrested and interrogated,
when he confessed to another £197,000 obtained by deception. For
this crime, which shook the City, he was ordered to be hung, at a time
when every year between thirty and forty people were executed for
forgery. The embezzling official, however, was fortunate to escape the
gallows and continued as a prisoner at Newgate until at least 1814
where, according to a press report, he 'lived a comparatively splendid
life'. When an American visitor, Louis Simond, saw him there in 1811,
he described the celebrity prisoner as 'playing merrily' with a printer
incarcerated for striking for higher wages.

In an even more sensational case, the reformed entrepreneur blew
the whistle on Benjamin Walsh, another lottery broker and Member
of Parliament for Wootton Bassett who had defrauded the Solicitor-
General, Sir Thomas Plomer, of £16,000 in a stock market scam.
Walsh, who had acted as stockbroker to Sir Thomas for many years,
was desperate to save his wife Mary and seven children from starvation
after being made bankrupt, with his partner Nesbitt, following the
failure of their city of London property lottery. For two years the

impoverished MP did every thing he could to make ends meet; he repeatedly pleaded with the Prime Minister, Spencer Perceval, for a government post, though his letters were not even answered, he auctioned off his entire picture collection, and he begged from friends and relatives. Nor was he able to make much money from stockbroking. In the great financial crash of July 1810, many City firms plunged into bankruptcy as a result of unwise speculations in South America and Spain, 'the consequences of a great number of persons who had, by paper credit, lived expensively without real property,' according to the diarist Joseph Farington.

At his wit's end, Walsh stole most of the £20,000 entrusted to him by Sir Thomas to buy government debentures and Exchequer bills and fled by mail coach to the West Country under the name of Wallis in a bid to escape to America, having bought £11,000 of American stock. The theft was discovered and a Bow Street runner called Adkins, with John Jenkins, legal representative of the Solicitor General, set off in a chaise and four in hot pursuit, finally apprehending the fugitive at Wynn's Hotel in Falmouth where he was waiting for a ship to take him across the Atlantic. Even then the deluded fraudster, as he later revealed in a letter to his brother, hoped his client would not make the matter public 'especially that it should not get into the *Morning Post*' as his wife was within seven days of giving birth and the shock of seeing it would kill her. Unfortunately for him, Bish, who had helped reveal the City lottery disaster and Walsh's role in creating a false market during it, happened to be staying at the same hotel and quickly heard of the arrest. Immediately, the arch-publicist dashed off a letter to his old acquaintance, James Perry, editor of the *Morning Chronicle*, the leading Whig daily newspaper. This was published on the ominous date of Friday 13 December 1811.

Bish wrote, 'I purposely passed through the room, which is a passage room to my bed-chamber, shortly indeed, five minutes after he was taken, and he was then walking up and down in a great agitation of mind. It is said that he has been guilty of some fraud towards Sir

T. Plomer, the Solicitor-General, to the amount of £16,000 but you, I dare say, know more about it than we do here.' The letter boasted, 'It is rather strange that I should have been the first to detect and expose Mr. W in 1808, and, also, by chance, the first person to hear of his being taken at so distant a port.' That did not make him popular with Walsh, who denounced Bish bitterly as 'an arch fiend' for making such 'a pretty story of it in the Newspapers'. At his crowded Old Bailey trial, where the MP appeared to be increasingly deranged, Walsh was convicted of felony on 18 January 1812, but later received a royal pardon which freed him from Newgate. MPs, however, voted by a large majority to expel him from Parliament, which he left still convinced Bish was the main cause of his downfall.

Another fraudster MP Bish helped bring to justice was Lord Cochrane, who had been a brilliant naval commander during the Napoleonic wars, second only to Lord Nelson. In 1814, he was accused with his crooked uncle Andrew Cochrane-Johnstone, MP for a rotten borough, and a former naval pay clerk called Butt of creating a false market on the Stock Exchange. They were alleged to have circulated a false rumour, through staging the excited arrival in London on 21 February of a bogus army officer from the battlefield, that the French were defeated and Napoleon killed, thus making themselves a gross profit of £10,000 during the consequent boom in government stock known as Omnium. At this time financial regulation hardly existed, the idea of insider trading was unknown and planting rumours was rife. But the Exchange, which had only recently produced its first code of conduct and was attracting men of real integrity, was determined to defend its credibility and reputation and to protect investors in Omnium. That is why, under the leadership of the pioneering actuary David Ricardo and the astronomer Francis Baily, supported by senior members including Bish, it acted swiftly once the first suspicions were raised, setting up a committee of enquiry into the share dealings. Within days the committee produced a preliminary report which was read out to the entire Stock Exchange and, at the instigation of Bish and others, who had successfully defeated a move to keep the findings secret, 600 copies were printed for general circulation. The false profits made by Joseph Fearn and other brokers acting for Lord Cochrane and his accomplices were entrusted in escrow to Bish and two other trustees pending further investigations. In vain did the beleaguered popular naval hero attack the committee, accusing it of collaborating with the government in order to smear him and doubting its motivation. It is true the initial enquiries seemed to rely on rumour. 'Mr. Bish was sent for,' record the minutes of the Exchange's governing body for 5 March 1814, 'and said he had heard from Mr. Philips who had heard from Mrs. Breton to whom it had been communicated by Mr. Sharpe that Mr. Fearn had said to him (Mr. Sharpe) that there was a circumstance going forward which if it took place he should make his fortune on 21 February.' Enough solid evidence was gathered, however, for the conspirators to be committed for a packed trial which was preceded by a vicious propaganda war in posters, press and pamphlets. Cochrane, who did not take the proceedings seriously and failed to attend, was traumatised to be found guilty and sentenced to an hour in the pillory, later commuted, a year in jail, a fine of £1,000, and expelled from both the House of Commons and the navy. Most humiliating was the manner of his expulsion from the Order of the Bath. He suffered a harsh medieval ceremony whereby, at midnight, his banner was torn down from the walls of King Henry VII's chapel in Westminster Abbey and kicked down the abbey steps into the dust, while a pair of spurs were hacked off the heels of a man standing as proxy for the disgraced sea warrior. Even Napoleon, exiled on the island of Elba, protested against this treatment. Fifty years later Cochrane was still protesting his innocence.

These high profile cases, combined with the steady emergence of his brand, turned the upwardly mobile Bish into a national figure. He was invited to Royal soirees, where the celebrated dandy Beau Brummell called him affectionately 'The Bish', no mean compliment, as the dictator of the London fashion scene usually affected a disdain for the City. Perhaps it was down to his love of playing the lottery with the Duchess of York. Bish was one of the guests at the spectacular Carlton House ball the Prince of Wales held in June 1811 to celebrate his accession as Prince Regent after his father King George III was declared insane. He joined the foreign princes, ambassadors, peers, government ministers, politicians, generals, and other notables who ate from a £61,340 gold dinner service on a two-hundred-foot-long table with a silver stream along which swam real fish. Dancing did not end until 4.30 a.m., prompting one guest, Lord Lonsdale, to declare, 'I was never so tired in my life.' He also regularly featured in the social columns, and invitations were eagerly awaited to his own parties where politicians, businessmen and society figures mingled. Even his arrival at fashionable resorts such as Buxton, Brighton and Edinburgh won a mention; the *Caledonian Mercury* of 2 October 1813 reports the arrival of 'Bish Esq and family from London' at Walker's Hotel in the Scottish capital, alongside news of the departure of the Chancellor of the Exchequer Nicholas Vansittart and his wife.

Rarely was Bish out of the news. Typical was his involvement in what must be the strangest episode in British theatrical history: the 1809 Old Price riots at Covent Garden. The previous year the theatre had burnt down, and when it was rebuilt the management put up prices in the pit from three shillings and sixpence to four shillings and installed many private boxes for the gentry and nobility, drastically cutting down the space for the cheaper seats. This outraged ordinary theatregoers and they started what became known as the 'Sixpenny War'. For sixty-seven nights from Monday 18 September scores of them disrupted performances with a surreal ritual called the Old Price Dance whereby they rose, turned their backs on the actors and then, with slow measured steps, stomped their legs in unison from left to right all the while bellowing 'O.P', 'O.P'. Others rang bells, blew horns, shook rattles, let pigs loose, fought with the constables and insulted their social superiors sitting in the boxes. So enjoyable was this mad nightly dance that it became more popular among the audience than the official action on stage. In a desperate attempt to restore order, the owner John Kemble, whose smart house in Great Russell Street beside the British Museum was repeatedly attacked, and the manager James Brandon hired thugs led by a Jewish prize-fighter called Daniel Mendoza to beat up the protestors as soon as they started their antics. Hundreds of free tickets were handed out to anyone thought likely to help the gang quash the disturbances, but, when challenged, Brandon vehemently denied doing so.

In his role as white knight, Bish spotted the lie, could prove it and helpfully publicised it in the press, provoking anonymous letters threatening him with injury or death. These he dismissed with a curt, 'They meet the contempt they deserve.' Many applauded his action. There appeared among the colourful placards brandished at the OP Dance – variously stating 'Oppose Shylock and the Jews', 'Fair play and fair prices' and 'The public voice will not be silenced by foul means' – a new placard which proclaimed 'BISH for Ever, MENDOZA Never'. Just before Christmas, the management caved in to the demands of the rioters. Brandon, who had so heavy-handedly co-ordinated the anti-OP campaign, was sacked, prices for admission to the pit were lowered to 1808 levels and the hated boxes torn out. It was a much happier outcome for the campaigning Bish than his son's short and ill-fated ownership of Drury Lane Theatre twenty years later.

At the same time as his excursions into public controversy, Bish was laying down the principles which made his selling techniques so effective at a time when chancing your luck on the lottery was becoming increasingly popular. By 1807 taxes had risen dramatically to fund the wars with the French. Markets fell and bankruptcies loomed as Napoleon, controlling most of Europe, was able to impose a trade blockade against Britain from Spain to Russia. As in other great credit crunches, people turned to the lucky draw in the hope of easing money troubles. Bish's basic technique was that sales pitches must appeal blatantly to greed. He was under no illusions that his customers acted from philanthropic motives, however much he himself might subscribe to charitable organisations, frequently appearing as a steward at their grand annual dinners. This is diametrically opposed to the way the UK National Lottery now tries to pull in punters. True, Camelot started with 'It Could Be You' adverts, an approach Bish would certainly have applauded, but has since swung in to emphasising its good causes role. Contrast this to the handbill, called *THE ALCHYMIST, or the Art of Making Money*. It declares:

> BISH's agent in this Town will put you in the way of placing yourself in either of the following enviable situations – you may buy a House and Land, and set up your Carriage – Enjoy domestic happiness, the society of friends, and never fear creditors – Live well, provide for your family, and escape poverty.

His famous plug *The Lottery Alphabet* is typical.

> A stands for All who for Affluence wish,
> B means Be sure Buy a Ticket of BISH,
> C Cash in plenty by BISH you may gain;
> D Don't Delay soon a Chance to obtain;
> E shows that Every One, if he is wise,
> F would Find out where to purchase a Prize
> G Gives the place; it is 4, in Cornhill...

Another rhyme read:

> The Bish for my money, I say,
> The likes of him never was known, sir:
> As Brulgruddery says in the play,
> That man's the philosopher's stone, sir
>
> Then what shall we do for this man,
> Who makes all your fortunes so handy?
> Buy his Tickets as fast as you can
> And drink him in Drops of Brandy

Self-confidence is again evident in a slightly oddly worded handbill of 1809 which proclaimed: 'If you are a man struggling to get through the world, or surrounded by crosses; or if you wish to lay a fortune for your children, go to BISH or his agents, who may make you independent, and above the frowns of the world.'

A Valentine Lottery of 1810 said:

And Bish is the Prize-Master, who sells most of them well
At Charing Cross, No. 9, or Blue Coat Boys, Cornhill;
Four Thousand Twenties, Five and Twenties, Thirties, Forties
  too,
He more has sold than all the Trade, and he'll sell one to you

A Lottery Song of 1803 proclaimed:

I say messmate, avast! Never talk of a cruise!
I've a voyage worth twenty, and twenty to choose!
A fig for Gravenny – at Boney cry pish! –
Come and enter with me under Commodore BISH.
Commodore BISH
At them both may cry pish!
Come and enter with me under Commodore BISH

Always with a sharp eye to the main chance, Bish took advantage of every possible opportunity to find a publicity angle. The 1809 visit to Britain of the Persian envoy, Mirza Abul Hasan, a popular and exotic society figure painted by the fashionable portrait artist Thomas Lawrence and described by the essayist Charles Lamb as 'the principal thing talked of now' was cheekily exploited in a song beginning 'The Persian Ambassador's come to town...'. It goes on to list his visits to the Court of George III, the Opera, dinner at the East India Company, Bank of England and ends with a visit 'To Bish's, a lottery ticket to buy,' where, according to the song, the famous lottery office keeper 'Wouldn't so impolite be as to sell him a blank'. The Ambassador leaves Britain saying:

Johnny Bull, thank ye for me;
With a Parlez vous, Voulez vous,
Bish I'll remember you

This was a technique his son, Tom, was later to emulate. In 1818 he took advantage of the three Royal Weddings that year, including that of the future mother of Queen Victoria, Princess Victoria of Saxe-Coburg, to the Duke of Kent, to publish a ditty called '3 ROYAL WEDDINGS and 3 £30,000 PRIZES'. With unerring instinct, he linked the three to declare:

Three Royal Weddings there shall be
To meet the Nation's wishes, Oh!
And Prizes, Thirty Thousands, Three
And these you'll meet at BISH's O

Napoleon, inevitably, featured prominently as pantomime villain in the seductive ads. One began:

Buonaparte's Cuirassiers were formed and armed with weapons to destroy the independence of nations. BISH's cuirassiers are formed and armed with manifestoes to secure the independence of every reader who is invited to purchase ... players now have an opportunity to obtain in a single hour, wine for life, and independence for ever.

The parallels with modern advertising are striking. A much broadcast television ad for the HSBC bank began: 'Eight is a lucky number for the Chinese. Eight is the interest rate HSBC pays...'. Two hundred years earlier a typical Bish newspaper ad ran:

In the old Roman Kalendar the lucky days were marked with Silver Letters: In Bish's Kalendar of Fortune they are marked with Capitals of Gold, and in the propitious month of April they have been marked with Showers of Gold; for in April, Bish sold all the Prizes of Thirty Thousand...

Another, promoting a lottery drawn on Saint Swithin's Day was headlined 'A SHOWER OF WINE!!!' And, somewhat blasphemously, suggested the entrepreneur could turn water into wine. It began:

> The WATERY SAINT on that day (15 July) did not shower down the usual favours, but our old friend BISH enabled him to shower WINE, instead of WATER, all over the United Kingdom; as it will be recollected, he added, as a Contractor for the last Lottery, Sixty Four Pipes of Wine, in Four Prizes

As the business grew, powered by highly intelligent selling, his son, universally known as Tom, became an effective partner, enthusiastically learning the tricks of the trade from his father whom he was later to surpass. Their relationship was affectionate and close. The pair became a well-known double act and featured in satirical prints. One 1809 etching portrayed them as 'Old Tom Puff' and 'Young Tom Puff' alongside an imitation banknote with a humorous text that mocked lotteries. Young Tom Puff was admitted to the Stock Exchange in 1806 at the age of twenty-eight where he built up a profitable portfolio in Navy bonds, India bonds, Exchequer Bills and Consols (government stock) and developed many useful contacts. Progressively, he began to be responsible for the increasingly complex and extremely lucrative lottery contracts, taking over the second office at 9 Charing Cross in 1813. As his father declined due to ill health, he effectively ran the family's entire commercial empire which by the time of his father's death at the age of sixty-three in December 1815 was estimated to be worth £200,000 (£10 million in today's money). This was despite setbacks such as the loss two years earlier of their lucrative seven-storey Commercial Hall building in Skinner Street near the old Fleet market, which fire razed to the ground one spring night. The obituarists seemed to have forgotten, or forgiven, his early misdemeanours; the leading Irish newspaper, *Freeman's Journal,* described him as 'a most eminent Stock Broker and Lottery Contractor distinguished for his activity intelligence and the most inflexible integrity'. A cynic might argue this accolade was due reward for the acres of lottery advertising the Bishes had bought over a quarter of a century.

Marketing sleight of hand stressed continuity, glossing over the inconvenient fact that Bish Senior was fading from the picture, with the occasional advert during his final months reminding everyone that 'Bish' had been in existence for thirty years. One, in the usual florid prose, congratulated all prizewinners 'who have participated in that unexampled good fortune which has for a period of upwards 30 years attended those who have favoured Bish's offices with a preference'. So seamless was the handover from father to son and so strong was the brand that social historians and some modern academics have assumed there was but one Thomas Bish.

An engraver's design for the heading of a 1813 lottery handbill

Enigmatic pictorial puzzles grabbed the attention. *Above left solution:*
'Time is on the wing, and Flies to shape in Fortune's Favours, 14th
June - Behold her Treasures unlocked.' *Above right solution:* 'If you
are a man struggling to get through the world, or surrounded by
crosses; or if you wish to lay by a fortune for your children, go to
BISH or his agents, who may make you independent, and above the
frowns of the world.'

CHAPTER THREE

Like Father, Like Son

How did the son Tom Bish manage to pull so far ahead of his twenty-five competitors to become the indisputably dominant broker, and achieve national fame? The answer lies in a trinity of a strong strategic brain, an infinite capacity for taking pains, and astonishingly bold showmanship. It is exceedingly rare for one person to possess all these qualities, and the combination, directed to making money, explains his extraordinary success as an outstanding entrepreneur and genuinely original communicator. Central to this was his utter self-belief and sheer cheek, characteristics shared by all successful showmen from Phineas Barnum to Richard Branson. Nowhere is this better illustrated than in a 'news item' he planted in the *Morning Chronicle* to promote one of his lucky draws, where the pioneer of puffery had the gall to announce, 'It has become the practice of late to begin paragraphs about some popular intelligence and then introduce the Lottery which has very properly disgusted many who are angry of being, as it were, taken in.' For his part, he disdained 'any such artificial aid' since tickets were cheaper and prizes more plentiful than for many years. With a disingenuousness that is breathtaking Bish concludes 'no puff is necessary to sell the few remaining tickets'. In the years that followed he was to drive puffery to unprecedented heights.

Bish operated two of the most well-known lottery houses at 4

Cornhill, which was considerably enlarged in 1817, and at 9 Charing Cross, boastfully described as 'the luckiest offices in the Kingdom'. There was some truth in this claim as he initiated the technique of drumming up interest by offering ever larger prizes. Indeed, one ad claimed, 'For the trifling risk of £4 – 10s someone must get upwards of £20,000.'

In the late twentieth century, Camelot used a similar pitch to launch the UK National Lottery in its brilliantly successful 'It Could Be You' marketing campaign. The young man, eager to outdo his father, was soon offering prizes of £30,000, sometimes three in the same draw, and marketing them as an 'attractive and unprecedented novelty'. This ploy still works wonderfully well today, the bigger the prize the more tickets are bought. That is why a plan for a world lottery with £500 million jackpots, which sounds so ridiculously over the top, is bound to succeed.

On 14 April 1815, the day before the draw, he published adverts under the headline:

WONDERFUL RICH WHEEL. They said
Buy Three Tickets, you may gain £90,000
Buy Two Tickets, you may gain £60,000

Ticket No. 2657 won one fortunate player a prize of £40,000. This prompted large advertisements in all national and regional newspapers from Exeter to Edinburgh, with Bish boasting 'such a continuation of luck is unparalleled in the history of lotteries'. He also claimed that to publish all the prizes he sold 'would require more volumes than the Statutes at large'. Hyperbole was always his forte. So was a solid brass neck; on one occasion, seriously misleading claims were made in a series of adverts which he airily dismissed as 'trifling typographical errors' when they were pointed out. Yet he also went to great lengths to give 'my friends the public' what he believed they wanted, (even if they did not know it themselves) through a primitive form of market research. Letters were sent out to selected regular players asking their advice on how the increasingly complex and sophisticated game could be improved still further. He is reported in *The Times* of 25 July 1820 as saying, 'I have this day contracted with the Government for 20,000 tickets to be drawn in one or two lotteries – and I have responded to suggestions from the public in drafting the scheme.'

Prizes became yet larger. The defeat of France in 1815 had made Britain the world's richest nation, and money was flowing. In the lottery of 7 November that year, there was 'a magnificent novelty', heavily promoted in the newspapers, of three prizes of £50,000 and four prizes of £20,000. The ingenious gamester also increased cash prizes from stock prizes, began offering 'fancy' lucky numbers, sometimes for a five-shilling premium, and free gifts for the first blank ticket drawn in various categories. Just like today, draws were regularly refreshed with all kinds of novelties, the silliest being '12 Pipes of Port Wine held for 1,000 years, or longer if required'. This drew a torrent of letters from wine merchants all asking that their wine be recommended for the prize. But when the public began to tire of complicated gimmicks, he was the first to sense this and switch tack. An 1822 advert, headlined 'GOOD OLD ENGLISH LOTTERY SCHEME', promised 'the greatest novelty of all', a simple old-fashioned game with no novelties whatsoever reminiscent of 'the good olden time'.

Even the 1820 trial of Queen Caroline was used for a lottery handbill. The repeated answer 'non mi ricardo' ('I don't recollect') by the chief prosecution witness, Signor Majocchi, to all questions put to him had become a national catchphrase – on a par with 'Been there, done that, got the T-shirt.' Bish soon exploited this in a question and answer verse entitled *NON MI RICARDO OR A few Questions on a new Subject* (which happened to be the lottery). In it Signor Majocchi is asked for his opinion on the best draw and replies:

Non mi ricardo, read the Scheme,
One word will answer all your wish

'Tis BISH's plan, 'tis BISH's theme
It must be good, 'tis planned by BISH

Unlike the ponderous efforts of competitors like Sivewright, Webb and Carroll (who soon, however, began imitating his style), his snappy and imaginative announcements caught the public's imagination. Adverts promoting the 1821 New Year State Lottery, for example, featured quirky verse-speaking portraits of characters from plays such as *She Stoops to Conquer* and *Tom Thumb* being staged in London over Christmas.

The increasingly confident entrepreneur, only too aware that the game was played mainly in London, was careful to include Wales, Scotland and Ireland. A St. David's Day lottery drawn on Saturday 1 March 1817, with only 3,000 tickets and a top prize of £15,000, was promoted as the 'smallest lottery ever known'. Handbills in both Welsh and English portraying a druid playing a harp were distributed in towns throughout Wales. Headed 'To the Inhabitants of this Town' they began:

An Express from LONDON has just arrived. ... the Scheme has been so highly approved by the Public in London, and by the Welsh nation in particular, that it is expected the remaining Tickets will be insufficient to meet the wishes of the Nation at large. An immediate application is essentially necessary...

They were also thrust at everyone attending Welsh Fairs in London such as Lambeth. One, entitled *The Maid of Llangollen* explains why a Welsh couple bought a ticket. The verse runs:

They had kisses in plenty – but what were all these,
For kisses would not supply bread to the cheese
So John Morgan and Winifred both felt a wish
For a Lottery Ticket from THOMAS AP BISH

It was on posters stuck up everywhere in the Welsh capital for this lucky draw that Bish used a device Camelot later employed so brilliantly in its famous 1994 campaign that its ads were seen on average thirteen times by forty million adults: this was a large pointing finger – one of the most recognisable commercial images ever – but it was first seen on the streets of Cardiff nearly 200 years ago.

At the same time this draw was launched, Bish assured his customers through press notices that other draws would take place on St. Patrick's Day, St. George's Day and St. Andrew's Day. He also targeted middle-class women by placing regular puffs in the monthly advertising supplements to *The Lady's Magazine: or Entertaining Companion for the Fair Sex*.

Using local papers to target provincial players became increasingly important. One jingle, headed *News for Norfolk*, said in rather fractured verse:

> The County for Norfolk for ever!
> Where practiced the best weaving work is
> Whose Dumplings for fame beat were never
> That at Christmas provides us with Turkies
> Tickets from Dunham and Yallop, Goldsmiths, Norwich

Oxford's jingle was headed *A Puzzle for Oxford*:

> Ye Classic Collegians, so famed for your parts
> Who Doctor Degrees, and who Master all Arts
> Tickets Mrs. Rackstraw, Library, Oxford

Bristol's *Lucky Ned* was a little more bucolic:

> In Zummerzetshire I wur born and bred
> And the Parson he zays that my name bez NED
> Barry, Booksellers, Bristol

Another, captioned *The Cheshire Chance*, ran:

> GOOD People all of Cheshire, so fam'd for making Cheese
> Tickets from T Cutter, printer, Chester
> Kent got Fortune's Target
> Ye Bowmen of Kent, pray attend
> Tickets T Crane, hatter, Maidstone

And in Cornwall *BISH's Golden Mine*:

> Ye Miners of Cornwall, of me you may learn
> (if you've luck) all your Tin into Silver may turn
> Tickets, J Heard, Bookseller, Truro

Prose items also followed provincial themes such as this paragraph from the *Kent Times* of 5 February 1819:

> However the Kentish speculators may have been unfortunate in the article of hops this season, there are some articles in which they have been most fortunate, namely the selection of lucky numbers in the Lottery. ... Many prizes won by people living in Maidstone, Canterbury, Margate

Like his father, Tom was an effective lobbyist, well able to influence the provisions of the Lottery Bill which Parliament was required to pass each year. At a 1820 meeting with chancellor Vansittart, he personally persuaded him to drop a scheme whereby the government could deprive a lottery contractor of his licence without allowing the opportunity for a defence or explanation. He also helped to defuse attempts to nationalise lotteries and more than held his own against the venomous attacks of anti-lottery campaigner Lord Lyttelton, who once, under the shield of parliamentary privilege, denounced the lotto men as 'fraudulent and criminal men not more worthy of trust than hangmen and informers'. Bish responded with one of his magisterial newspaper letters, effectively accusing the intemperate peer of cowardice, challenging him to substantiate or withdraw and concluding 'the public must decide whether Disgrace attaches to the Accused or Accuser'. At the same time, he had to defend himself against the attacks of competitors, particularly Carroll, who accused him of deviously acquiring most of the prizes for his personal profit. 'Malignant efforts' and 'disgraceful falsehoods' were some of the politer epithets flung at him. His response was clearly equally robust. Carroll must have been smarting when he issued this statement, 'To expose duplicity and unmask hypocrisy is my object and I am not to be deterred from my purpose by PRIVATE THREATS and Public Calumny.' Quite what those threats were is not known, but the spat over the terms of one lottery in 1820 was sufficiently serious for Bish to break off a trip 'many hundreds of miles off' (it must be presumed either Ireland or Europe) to hurry back to London to deal with the potential damage to his reputation.

A long-standing Freemason, Bish was always very keen to protect his good name, which he did by playing an active role in a remarkable range of charitable and philanthropic associations, including the Society for the Suppression of Mendicity, St. Patricks's Benevolent Society, Friends of the National School Institution, the City of London General Pension Society, providing 'pensions for labourers and their widows within ten miles of London', and the Musical Fund for aged musicians and their families. When this last held its 22nd Anniversary Dinner at London's Freemasonry Tavern in 1824, clubbable Bish was a steward, as he was at so many other male-dominated society dinners, which were also useful business networking events. On this occasion, the wives were allowed to watch. 'The gallery was adorned by the presence of many ladies who appeared to take a lively interest in the bustling scene that was passing beneath them,' reported the *Morning Chronicle*.

Even more than his father, success turned Bish into a society figure whose traditional parties on the evening of each new lottery draw were crowded with fashionable politicians, businessmen and artists. He appeared in satirical prints such as the *Portrait of the Chancellor of the*

Exchequer, part of THE GALLERY OF THE PRESENT AGE series which the magazine *Bell's Life in London and Sporting Chronicle* published in 1825. The caption explains that the portrait:

> also features Rothschild, Joseph Hume, Crowds of spectators and Lord Bexley with a bible under one arm and a broken lottery wheel under another. He toddles towards a cabriolet supported on one side by Bish, the lottery contractor, and on the other by Mrs Fry, the dispenser of religious tracts.

His prominence owes much to the emergence of a culture of celebrity which helped to sell newspapers and periodicals then being printed in increasing numbers. Readers had a vociferous appetite for the doings of public figures like Byron, Mrs. Siddons, Edmund Kean and the clown Joey Grimaldi, whose unmistakable face was also used to sell a huge range of products from prints to pocket watches. By skilful manipulation of his image (romantic hero rather than overweight poseur with a club foot), Byron came to represent romance and adventure, becoming a celebrity at the age of twenty-four with the overnight success of his loosely autobiographical poem *Childe Harold's Pilgrimage*. Lady Caroline Lamb's famous description of the theatrical poet as 'mad, bad and dangerous to know' only served to increase his appeal. Likewise Tom Bish sold 'luck', his name being synonymous with it; fifteen years after his death in 1843 racehorses were still being named after him. More strategic than his father, the shameless young self-publicist revolutionised the use of writers, illustrators, and the very first advertising agents, using them in an integrated way which today is taken for granted in tightly focused marketing campaigns. Bish pioneered this holistic approach to communication disciplines with imagination, drive and intellectual vigour. It was his most original contribution to advertising.

Dame Fortune encourages excited lottery players in this 1810 handbill

Not everyone was impressed by the early advertising boom
(from *McLean's Monthly Sheet of Caricatures*, 1 March 1831)

"Nowadays, adverts are the only part of the papers you can believe"

CHAPTER FOUR

The Writers

Copywriters 200 years ago – mainly Grub Street hacks supplementing their meagre wages, redundant civil servants, unemployed governesses, educated spinsters, burnt-out playwrights and unsuccessful lawyers – would scarcely credit the money and status conferred on their counterparts today. Yet the talent to combine literary skill with selling a product in just a few lines was as rare then as it is now. No wonder so many future novelists such as Salman Rushdie, Scott Fitzgerald, Joseph Heller, Eric Ambler, Len Deighton, Peter Carey, Dorothy L. Sayers and Fay Weldon all started out as copywriters. As Aldous Huxley, no mean writer himself, once said, 'advertisements are one of the most interesting and difficult of modern literary forms'. Bish and Son were the first to grasp the possibilities of harnessing writing talent to commercial ends in order to produce imaginative advertisements. That is why they hired, either directly or indirectly through agents, talented people like the songwriter Robert Houlton, the wit and journalist Theodore Hook, the comic poet Thomas Hood and even Charles Lamb, to compose their lottery jingles.

Today, top creatives can earn a fortune, in contrast to their professional ancestors who were mostly paid a pittance and were seen, contemptuously (though not by the Bishes who appreciated their work), as hired hands, way down the social pecking order on a par with the kitchen maid, or worse. Their demeaning work was mocked. Charles Dickens satirised them in *The Old Curiosity Shop*; Mr. Slum, writer of jingles for 'the perfumer, the blacking markets ... the hatter, the old lottery house keepers' claims absurdly 'it's the delight of my life to have dabbled in poetry'. John Fairburn's *Quizzical Gazette Extraordinary*, an annual of mock advertisements like *Private Eye's* spoof Christmas advertising supplement, announced in its 1821 edition:

> LOTTERY LAUREAT WANTED – He must possess a sufficient poetical talent to undertake all the rhyming gullery, and be able to envelop Fraudulent Schemes in lucky hieroglyphic obscurity.

In his 1814 mock pastoral *Crambo*, George Daniel describes two bailiffs emptying out the pockets of a hack lying drunk in the gutter and finding 'not one single halfpenny in cash' but only lottery puffs and other 'literary trash'. Earlier, in a novel called *The Adventures of Dick Distich*, the satirist introduces another hack, Mr. Aristarchus, as 'a dirty miserable wretch, with no shirt, half a pair of breeches and a coat without sleeves ... who lives at the farthing pie-house in Saint Giles's'.

So marginalised were they that *Scribbleomania*, an 1815 verse satire on every class of writing, clearly believed they were beyond parody and not worth even a mention in the main text of the Miscellaneous Writers chapter; puffs for Robert Warren's shoe polish and Bish's lottery are simply reproduced as footnotes. Today, the despised hacks would be celebrated in award-winning television drama series such as *Mad Men* about the lives of New Yorkers working in Madison Avenue advertising.

The ancient scribes were just as creative, and rather more productive, churning out by the yard jingles, comic verses, mock heroic burlesques, fables, pastiches, dialogues, mini-dramas, nursery rhymes, anecdotes, ads disguised as news stories, riddles, puns, jokes and catchy slogans, just as accomplished as anything produced in the era of 'Guinness is

Best,' 'What We Want is Watneys,' 'Players Please' and 'Go To Work on an Egg'.

They would have been equally at home in the golden age of radio jingles during the 1950s and 1960s which created such classic once-heard-never-forgotten songs as 'We are the Ovaltineys! Little Boys and Girls!' Proof positive of their talent is the evidence of London magistrate Patrick Colquhoun to a House of Commons committee in 1816. 'The public was encouraged to resort to the lottery by the most captivating devices which ingenuity, uncontrolled by moral rectitude, can invent,' he told the MPs. Others agreed that the puffs worked; William Hazlitt complained, 'your spare cash is conjured clean out of your pocket,' the *Gentleman's Magazine* described them as 'baneful and fascinating temptations to crime,' and Lord Lyttelton harrumphed in Parliament about 'gross and contemptible fabrications'. Since then complex social and economic changes have created a culture which rewards innate talent and ability rather than class and inherited wealth, though whether someone who dreams up catchphrases for selling tampons is worth paying fifty times more than a nurse is debatable.

But in the days when the Bish brand was putting advertising on a professional footing, it was a buyer's market. The number of daily, evening and Sunday newspapers, journals and magazines published in London, Europe's largest and richest city housing more than a million people, had doubled to 180 in the twenty years to 1826. Annual sales reached seventeen million. Even before this dramatic expansion, foreign visitors were amazed. 'It seems about 100,000 newspapers are printed and sold every day in England,' recorded the shrewd Persian envoy to King George III's court, Abul Hasan, in an 1809 diary entry. 'How extraordinary that today's newspapers will have no value tomorrow – except as toilet paper!' And, of course, as advertising.

'Advertisements flowed in beyond bounds,' recalled Daniel Stuart, editor of the *Morning Post,* of a money-spinning golden age when out of the entire media only the *Sheffield Iris* was prepared to lose profits by refusing lottery advertisements on moral principle. Some editors like Leigh Hunt of the reforming *The Examiner* banned all advertisements on political principle, fearing they might compromise editorial independence. When William Cobbett launched his radical journal *The Porcupine* in 1800, he too banned dodgy ads, promising 'Not a single quack advertisement will on any account be admitted.' Most publishers happily accepted them, especially during general elections when political advertising was charged at a much higher rate than commercial inserts, increasing profits by as much as seventy per cent.

There were still too many writers for the work available. In Pierce Egan's 1821 bestselling *Real Life in London*, which details the picaresque adventures of London dandy Bob Tallyho and his country cousin Tom Dashall, the two heroes stumble upon a fifty-year-old poorly dressed literary writer sitting disconsolately on a bench in St. James's Park. He explained he had lost his job as a government clerk without compensation or pension as his post was too far down the bureaucratic scale to qualify. That would certainly have been true, since Treasury rules on redundancy payments discriminated disproportionally against the lower ranks; during a lay-off in 1827 the most senior government employee received a very generous pension of ten-twelfths of his salary and the most junior a miserly payment of £120. Asked how he now made his living, the dispirited hack replied: 'From puffing – writing rhyming advertisements for certain speculative and successful candidates for public favour in various associations, for instance, eulogizing the resplendent brilliancy of Jet or Japan Blacking – the wonderful effects of Tyrian-Dye and Macassar Oil in producing a luxuriant growth and changing the colour of the hair, transforming the thinly scattered and auburn tresses of youth … Sir, I am reduced to this occasional humiliating employment, derogatory certainly to the dignity of literature, as averting the approach of famine.'

Revealing the astonishing output then common, he added 'I have written for a certain Blacking Manufacturer about 200 different productions on the subject of his unparalleled Jet … the remuneration is of a very trifling nature for such mental labour'. Scandalised by what he had heard, Bob exclaimed, 'I would not, were I a bricklayer's labour exchange situations with this unfortunate literary hack – this poor devil of mental toil and precarious result, who depends for scanty subsistence on the caprice of his more fortunate inferiors.'

Not all were so badly paid. Robert Houlton, one-time editor of the *Morning Herald* and writer of songs, librettos and comic operas, took the corporate shilling of the lottery contractors following a spell in the Fleet prison for debt caused by running up huge medical bills. One contractor, Thomas Cope, who only six years previously had defaulted on the Stock Exchange, spent a massive £36,000 (more than £1 million today) on 'advertising, pole-men and travelling expenses' to promote the lottery of 1809. Under Salaries and Petty Charges on his balance sheet there appears the entry 'Dr. Houlton, for literary services (aka writing lottery puffs, at the age of seventy) for £129-8-0.' This was considerably more than the £38-17-6 paid to the famous Cruikshank studio for painting designs for lottery tickets that year. His songs and ballads such as *Blithsome Cherry* and *Fair Rose of the Grove* were hits at the popular Vauxhall Pleasure Gardens bordering the River Thames in Kennington. So he, at least, had a decent income.

Probably Houlton could command higher fees through his earlier reputation as an up-and-coming playwright. He had written the prologue to *Crotchet Lodge*, a farce performed at the Theatre Royal, Covent Garden in 1795, and the epilogue to the comedy *The Bank Note or Lessons for Ladies* also put on there the same year. Lines in the latter production such as:

……. – kind friends support our cause
And oh! – Let's hear your rattle of applause

are hardly Shakespearean, but this medical student-turned-writer obviously had some talent, which culminated in the 1800 staging of a two-act comic opera called *Wilmore Castle* at Drury Lane Theatre. James Hook, who wrote more than 2,000 songs for Vauxhall over a

fifty year period and was elder brother of Theodore Hook (another
writer of lottery jingles), composed the music. After running for five
nights to mixed reviews it was taken off, Houlton afterwards bitterly
complaining of a concerted campaign against the production. He
never, however, lost his affection for the advertising industry which
provided his living in later years; he happily added his name to a list
published in 1801 of people endorsing the Golden Pills of Life and
Beauty produced by one Jane Wynne of Trowbridge, Wiltshire, alleged
to cure all ailments and 'particularly recommended as a useful Medicine
during Pregnancy, by greatly relaxing the bowels'.

Like Houlton, Theodore Hook wrote farces, melodramas and
librettos for comic operas, the first for a show composed by his father
called *What Can Beauty Do?* He was just sixteen and it earned him £50.
He became famous as an innovator hoaxer, fraudster and, above all,
as an outstanding editor of the immensely influential and scurrilous
weekly periodical *John Bull*, set up in 1820 to lampoon Queen Caroline,
and which the Whigs repeatedly but unsuccessfully tried to suppress
with libel actions. Hook was a versifier of such brilliance that the poet
Samuel Coleridge and the playwright Richard Sheridan both compared
him to Dante. Today, this genius would be a famous stand-up comic
sweeping up all the prizes at the Edinburgh Fringe. Once, on seeing
a defaced wall placard bearing the slogan 'WARREN'S B------------
(for *BLACKING*)', Hook remarked without hesitation, 'What ought
to follow is lacking.' On another occasion, he was entertaining on a
pianoforte when Mr. Winter, a well-known Inspector of Taxes was
announced to the room.

With abnormally fast wit, Hook immediately sang:

Here comes Mr. Winter, Inspector of Taxes
I'd advise ye to give him whatever he axes
I'd advise ye to give without any flummery
For tho his name is Winter, his actions are summary

Diarist Charles Greville recalls the quipster starring at a Roehampton dinner party in 1834. 'Last night he was very brilliant,' he wrote. 'Each lady gave him a subject such as the 'Goodwood Cup', the 'Tithe Bill', one 'could not think of anything' which he dashed off and sang stanzas innumerable, very droll, with ingenious rhymes and excellent hits, his eyes begetting occasion for his excellent wit, for at every word of interruption or admiration, every look or motion, he indulged in a digression, always coming back to one of the themes imposed upon him. It is a tour de force, in which I believe he stands alone and it is certainly wonderfully well worth hearing and uncommonly amusing.' The liberal editor Leigh Hunt recounted a similar occasion at the Sydenham home of Mr. Hill, proprietor of the *Monthly Mirror*, where Hook came unexpectedly to dinner and displayed a 'really surprising' talent at the pianoforte for parodying both music and words. 'He knew nothing of the company or its conversation', he wrote, 'yet he ran his jokes and his verses upon us in the easiest manner, saying something characteristic of everybody, or avoiding it with a pun'. The stand-up musical comedian Tim Minchin would be the nearest modern equivalent. Another time a friend drove down with him to Epsom and recalled afterwards 'during the whole journey he kept up a regular running fire of pun, anecdote and improviso'. As the gig reached the turnpike Vauxhall Bridge, Lennox remarked 'I wonder if this bridge pays?' His companion shot back, 'Go over it and you will be tolled.'

Hook's uncanny ability to churn out satirical verses, squibs and comic songs on demand made him a natural copywriter, as did the quirky imagination he displayed during the course of his chequered career. Typical of his pranks was the notorious Berners Street Hoax of 1809 when he deceived the Lord Mayor of London, Governor of the Bank of England, chairman of the East India Company, the Duke of Gloucester and 4,000 others into attending a non-existent soiree at the Berners Street home of the unfortunate Mrs. Tottenham, whom he disliked. At the same time there arrived cartloads of coal, curtains, organs, pianofortes, and furniture, along with cooks bearing massive wedding cakes, undertakers with coffins, draymen with beer barrels, forty fishmongers carrying lobsters and forty butchers carrying legs of mutton. This madness attracted huge crowds and widespread public disorder. Hook was never punished, since his involvement could not be proved. He was not so fortunate during his next adventure in Mauritius where he was, bizarrely, appointed accountant-general without any business qualifications, and ran up an unexplained shortfall of at least £30,000 during his four-year tenure of office. Although he managed to avoid criminal prosecution, the Treasury seized his property and, from 1823-1825, he was imprisoned for his liability for the loss. Characteristically, he dismissed the episode with the bon mot, 'If they wanted the balance regular, they should have looked for a man with more weight.'

Throughout his escapades Hook made a good living from writing not only satire, which scared the Whig aristocrats, but acclaimed novellas, biographies, farces and innumerable articles in journals and newspapers from *The Times* to the *Sierra Leone Gazetter*. With six children to support by his live-in lover Mary Anne Doughty, he could never lay down his pen, which is why advertising work was always welcome as a side-line; he is listed, for instance, as a contact in the 1822 address book of London-based Charles Barker, one of the first advertising agencies.

Like fellow workaholic and alcoholic, the illustrator George Cruikshank who both produced illustrations for lottery handbills and anti-lottery drawings for evangelical tracts, Hook also ran with the hare and rode with the hounds. For creatives, then, that was entirely normal; they needed money and took commissions from any paymaster.

After Parliament abolished the state lottery, Hook lampooned Bish's audacious spinning in *John Bull* on 10 December 1826, enquiring:

Shall we never feel more a pecuniary wish,
Puff'd up by the florid inflations of Bish?

The rhyme continued:

> Bish used to print paragraphs artfully penn'd –
> We saw not his aim till we read to the end –
> 'Great news from abroad!' – 'A suspicion of treason!'
> 'A mermaid exhibiting just in the season!'
> Through foreign news, mermaid, or radical plotter, he
> Always contrived to get round to the Lottery

Yet only a few months later the flexible scribbler, on behalf of Bish, was spinning the lottery himself, urging punters to buy tickets in the last draw before abolition removed forever their chance of making a fortune. On that occasion, the 'florid inflation', printed in newspapers and in handbills distributed all over London, read:

> Run, Neighbours, Run, the LOTTERY'S expiring,
> When Fortune's merry wheel it will never turn more;
> She now supplies all NUMBERS you're desiring,
> ALL PRIZES, NO BLANKS and TWENTY THOUSANDS
> FOUR

> *Haste, Neighbours, haste, the Chance will never come Again ....*

Hook appears here to be recycling the chorus line of his recent verses mocking the financial bubbles that burst into the credit crunch crisis of 1825:

> Run, neighbours, run, you're just in time to get a share...
> No matter where the project lies, so violent the mania
> In Africa, New Providence, Peru or Pennsylvania!
> Run, neighbours, run, you're just in time to get a share,
> In all the famous bubbles that amuse John Bull

Perhaps the most famous copywriter was a brilliant essayist, playwright, journalist, poet and one of the first to grasp the genius of the visionary poet William Blake: Charles Lamb. Friend of Coleridge,

Wordsworth, Keats, Hazlitt and Shelley, he is best known for his *Tales of Shakespeare* which he co-wrote with his sister Mary and has never been out of print. But Lamb also wrote light-hearted verses and prose for Daniel Stuart at the *Morning Post* between 1802 and 1804, articles for James Perry at the powerful Whig daily the *Morning Chronicle* and political commentary for Leigh Hunt at the *Examiner* between 1810 and 1820. He later described the drudgery of knocking out newspaper jokes at sixpence a time as 'slavery' beyond anything devised by an Egyptian taskmaster, though he needed work to ward off the life-long bouts of depression caused by Mary infamously knifing their mother to death with a carving knife when he was twenty-one. Journalism was also light relief from his day job as a clerk (his sister hated anyone calling him that) at the bureaucratic accounts office of the East India House, logging details of shipments of tents, cotton indigo dyes, teas and spices. Although he was eventually promoted to a managerial post, most of his time there was spent scribbling away with five other clerks in a compartment called a 'Compound', housed within a large accountant's office. He was once asked for the meaning of the word and relied with typical caustic wit, 'it is a collection of simples'. The literary genius endured this mechanical work, as his friend Wordsworth described it, for thirty-three years from 1792, taking early retirement at the age of fifty with a generous pension equivalent to two-thirds of his salary. He told a confidant he would not return to the Compound even for a hundred thousand pounds, though he later admitted, 'I missed my old chains.'

Drink also helped to anaesthetise the daily grind, and it made him an alcoholic; on at least one occasion he was put into the stocks for drunken antics and jeered at – mental torture for such a sensitive soul. The dreariness and pettiness of office life, including jokey references to the 'addition of the Third Column of Cotton Wool', comes over brilliantly in an unpublished skit (lain forgotten in a strongbox deep in the archives of the India Office records at the British Library). Written in his beautifully neat copperplate hand, it is headed 'Rules and

directions to be observed by Mr. Chambers at the end of June 1823 ...
to obviate the inconvenience of my absence'.

Chambers is advised if he meets a Director in the passage, 'Do
not kick him, under pretence of not knowing who he was; for depend
upon it, however he may appear to be pacified with your apology, he
will secretly treasure up the remembrance of the wrong you did him.'
He is further advised not to let 'Gardiner the messenger treat you with
that hauteur, with which he is too apt to behave towards his seniors',
not to believe 'above half what Plumley tells you', to give Rice long
accounts to copy 'because he loves them', not to intervene 'if you see
Rice and Dodwell ready to cut one another's throats' and to watch out
for the firelighters asking for their Christmas boxes prematurely, '...I
have known Drysdale in this manner imposed upon to give Christmas
boxes three or four times over'.

Although Lamb needed money to fund the parties which
compensated for his humdrum job, he took a romantic view of the
lottery, describing it as 'this most generous diffuser of universal
happiness' and had no qualms about promoting it. One of the first
advertising agents, James White, a school friend at Christ's Hospital,
whose Bluecoat boys traditionally drew the winning tickets from the
lottery wheels, persuaded him to write copy. That is evident from a
letter Mary Lamb wrote to Sarah Hazlitt in 1809. In it she said, 'A
man in the India House has resigned, by which Charles will get twenty
pounds a year; and White has prevailed on him to write some more
lottery-puffs. If that ends up in smoke, the twenty pounds is a sure
card, and has made us very joyful.' Twenty years later William Hazlitt,
in his essay *Of Patronage and Puffing* revealed that a talented friend had
been commissioned by Bish to write regular lottery advertisements,
but had had 'a parcel of samples returned on his hands as done in too
severe and terse a style'. Speculation that this was Lamb may, however,
be wrong since his writing is scarcely ever terse.

One lottery ad, which legend has it is by Lamb, though there is
no conclusive evidence, was placed by White's firm in *Bell's Weekly
Messenger* just before the turn of 1806. It read:

A SEASONABLE HINT, – Christmas gifts of innumerable descriptions will now pervade this whole kingdom. It is submitted whether any present is capable of being attended with so much good to a dutiful son, an amiable daughter, an industrious apprentice, or a faithful servant, as that of a SHARE of a LOTTERY TICKET, in a scheme in which the smallest share may gain near two thousand pounds.

Another, which I suspect from the punning style may be by Lamb (himself an enthusiastic card player) appears in a handbill advertising the January 1817 lottery, which Bish was organising. It is headed *A Hint to Speculators* and features as a visual aid four playing cards in red. It was printed by Frederick Gye, who produced so many of Bish's promotions. The text claims that the lottery is a game 'superior to Piquet, Quadrille, Whist, Loo, or Cribbage' which will make you 'as rich as a King.' It begins with an extended metaphor: 'If you would be Put in the way of playing your cards to advantage and would gain a Trump with little Hazard, I beg to point out to you a Speculation, by which, without a Brag, you may win the Game of Independence, and divide the honours among you, of Ease, Happiness and Prosperity.' Lamb enjoyed a reputation of being able to produce puns to order. Some were dreadful. His barrister friend Martin Burney once challenged him to make a pun on the name of Bish, claiming it was impossible to do so. The ingenious essayist shot back that only that morning he had visited Tom Bish in his room at the Stock Exchange and, on leaving it, was stopped by a broker who asked him jocularly whether Bish was still alive. (There were times when the lottery entrepreneur felt it prudent to keep a low profile). Lamb replied, 'Yes – he B (be) B (be) Bish-yet.'

A later ad, which has the whiff of Lamb about it, is a small handbill titled *Ambulator's Guide to the Land of Plenty*. This was distributed to drum up support for a Bish lottery starting on 30 August 1820. 'By purchasing a TICKET,' it declares 'you may reap a Golden Harvest in Cornhill and pick up by bullion in Silver Street; have an Interest

in Bank Buildings; possess a Mansion House in Golden Square; and
An Estate like a little Britain; pour red Wine down Gutter Lane;
never be in Hungerford Market; but all your life continue in May-fair.'
There could be another author, however. About this time Lamb took
under his wing an ambitious young man who later became a poet and
outstanding comic versifier, admired by literary figures from William
Wordsworth to Charles Dickens. 'As a punster, he is equal to Swift,'
claimed one contemporary. This was Thomas Hood, then tentatively
starting out on a career as a literary journalist which he supplemented
by hack work, including lottery puffs. Like most of his fellow aspiring
writers, he needed to earn money wherever he could once he had given
up his job at a City counting house. 'I am now obliged to turn the
amusing if I can, into the profitable,' he said in a letter to his friend
George Rollo. He knew James White from soirees at the Lambs. His
mentor Charles, whom he saw three evenings a week when they were
neighbours in Islington, collaborated with him on a range of writing
projects including dramatic productions. His talent for comic verse was
well suited to contemporary humorous advertising. And, like Lamb
and others, he feared that the abolition of the state lottery would kill
off the fledging profession of copywriting. Among the laments is an
affectionate ode to his early paymaster titled *To Thomas Bish Esq*, first
published by the *New Monthly Magazine* in 1827 as part of the *Odes and
Addresses to Great Men* series. It begins:

> My Bish, since fickle Fortune's dead
> Where throbs thy speculating head
> That hatch'd such matchless stories

The squib mourns his demise:

> No more thy name in column stares
> On the lurid reader unawares
> The voice of Fame is o'er!

It also warns 'the puff to others now belongs', citing Wright the champagne king, Henry Hunt the shoe blacking maker and Rowland the hair oil entrepreneur.

His son and daughter, who edited the first collection of their father's work, his first biographer Walter Jerrold and literary historians since have all assumed that Hood must have composed this playful burlesque. He did not. On his deathbed in 1845 he wrote to an autograph hunter, G. B. Webb, 'I did not write the lines on Mr. Bish, having at the time to fry some other fish'. Practically a comic rhyming couplet, proving he kept his sense of humour to the end. For good measure, he added, 'As I am going I know not where, if you want another Autograph, you must apply to my Heir.' So who did write it? Internal evidence points to Lamb, not least because of the comparisons between Bish, 'Charing Cross's Bonaparte' and Napoleon which Lamb had already used elsewhere. So convinced was the romantic poet, Samuel Taylor Coleridge, that his old friend had written the odes that he sent him a teasing letter: 'No! Charles, it is you. I have read them over again, and understand why you have anon'd the book.'

Contemporary rumours that other celebrated literary figures wrote for the lucky draw cannot, alas, be substantiated. Coleridge experimented with comic verses early in his career and, on one occasion, suicidal through money worries, he bought a ticket in the Irish game, which failed to win a prize. It did, however, inspire him to write a burlesque called 'To Fortune' which was published in the *Morning Chronicle* on 7 November 1793, earning him a guinea. Lord Byron himself was once accused of receiving £500 for writing advertisements for Day and Martin's blacking and replied facetiously, 'This is the highest compliment to my literary powers which I ever received.' If they, like Lamb, were tempted to sell their poetical souls to Bish and colleagues, they were exceptionally discreet about it.

A surprising number of other writers supplemented their income by being appointed, usually through political patronage, as lottery commissioners, who regulated the draw on behalf of the Government.

In 1797 the Prime Minister, William Pitt the Younger, gave one of these sinecures to the Tory satirist and autodidact William Gifford, son of a plumber who rose from poverty via an Oxford scholarship to become author of the *Baviard* and celebrated editor of the *Quarterly Review*. For this former shoemaker's apprentice, the streets were indeed paved with gold. Another Tory beneficiary was John Heriot, a former marine who turned to writing novels and started the highly successful *Sun* evening newspaper in 1793 with the support of Edmund Burke and secret funding from the Pitt Government to counteract 'the mischievous principles of revolutionary France'. He accepted a £350 a year clerkship in the Lottery Office in 1806, giving it up three years later for the idyllic post of Paymaster to the Leeward and Windward Islands, where he lived with his entire family.

Falling ticket sales, caused partly by the post-Napoleon economic recession and increasingly vociferous evangelical campaigns led by William Wilberforce, finally forced Parliament to abolish the state lottery, which had been a national institution for 132 years. Its last fling in 1826 was preceded by one of the most original and expensive advertising campaigns in history, which showered London with handbills and leaflets and blocked its streets with colourful processions and promotional carts. It was a sad time for the copywriters, heroes of the infant advertising industry which had been developed to market the draws.

An anonymous verse published in the *News of Literature* summed up their plight:

Woe unto us poor devils of the quill
For closed against us is one bounteous mart
No more shall we compose the sentence, terse,
Or hymn Tom Bish in floods of numerous verse.

CHAPTER FIVE

The Illustrators

Pablo Picasso, Henri Toulouse-Lautrec, John Everett Millais, Salvador Dali, Rene Magritte, Claude Monet, Aubrey Beardsley, Norman Rockwell, Ben Nicholson, Paul Nash, John Piper, Georgia O'Keefe, Andy Warhol, Jackson Pollock, Willem De Kooning, Jeff Koons – the roll-call of artists who have illustrated advertisements is long and impressive. Less well-known are the pioneers of this strange but profitable alliance between art and commerce. It was a stroke of genius that led Tom Bish to commission many professional contemporary artists like Robert Seymour, Luke Clennell, John Thurston and Robert Branston to liven up his lottery puffs. But the most brilliant artist he used was the great George Cruikshank, illustrator of Charles Dickens' *Oliver Twist* and *Nicholas Nickleby,* and one of the most original and productive graphic satirists ever. The art critic John Ruskin compared his etchings to Rembrandt. He began his career at the age of eight, designing lottery tickets and children's books for his father, the caricaturist Isaac Cruikshank, who taught him to etch and draw. None of these early works survives, 'having, of course, been destroyed long ago by the dear little ones who had them to play with,' he wrote in old age. He meant the eleven children he fathered with his mistress and former housemaid, Adelaide Attree. Hundreds of designs he produced for advertisements have survived, however. One design, commissioned by Tom Bish to help sell tickets for a lottery drawn on 5 and 18 October, 1817 at Coopers' Hall in the city of London, was later recycled as a satire on the Royal Family, which sold a sensational half million copies and so alarmed King George IV that he offered Cruikshank £100 to drop his ridicule. This was *Fortune's Ladder*, used on handbills and posters, which urged the reader to 'Take a Paddy's advice, and begin at the end' (i.e. read from bottom to top). There are ten rungs labelled from Deprivation to Exaltation, each with woodcut and jingle, telling the story of the rise from poverty to wealth of a married couple who buy a lottery ticket from Bish.

He used precisely the same device in *The Queen's Matrimonial Ladder*, the notorious illustrated pamphlet on the adultery trial of Queen Caroline which was issued with a cardboard ladder and produced in collaboration with the radical journalist and publisher William Hone. Marketed as a 'A National Toy', it displayed fourteen inch-high step scenes and illustrations in verse along with fourteen other cuts. One of them entitled 'Qualification' portrayed the monarch in his cups over the mocking lines:

> In love, and in drink, and o'ertoppled by debt
> With women, with wine, and with duns on the fret

Always in debt, Cruikshank never turned down any commission and churned out what the market wanted, a total of more than 6,000 separate prints over his working life. Nothing was ever wasted, like today; Steve Bell's 2008 award-winning cartoon showing Gordon Brown giving the thumbs up as he sinks into a brown creek is based on one of his original John Major satires. Similarly, the Ministry of Information, using the pioneering animation studio Halas & Batchelor, economically recycled graphic images in the stylish and surreal public information films it screened in cinemas throughout World War II. Hordes of moths honing in on badly stored clothes, and subliminally suggesting Nazi warplanes, in the film *Make Do and Mend* became hordes of angry

(TO BE READ FROM THE BOTTOM.)

The drift of this Ladder, to well comprehend,
Take a Paddy's advice and *begin* at the *end.*

(3)

She answer'd thus, "If
you are wise,
You'll try at BISH'S for
a Prize."
The thought inspir'd
with hope the man,
Who off to BISH's quickly
ran.
(*Go to No.* 4.)

(2)

"My dearest wife, the
times are bad,
And, as to Cash, it can't
be had,
In this sad plight, what
what shall we do ?
Or, pray, what plan can
we pursue ?"
(*Go to No.* 3.)

(1)

A wight, by poverty
oppress'd,
By duns and creditors
distress'd,
Thus to his dame in
dudgeon said,
While dreams of horror
fill'd his head.

(6)

Not long he waits, the
lucky youth
Who drew the Prize,
proclaims the truth,
And in his breast "fond
hopes arise,
It is a Twenty Thousand
Prize !"
(*Go to No.* 7.)

(5)

At home arriv'd, he tells
his dear,
And anxiously expects
to hear
The glorious, heart-in-
spiring sound,
"'Tis drawn, a Twenty
Thousand Pound !"
(*Go to No.* 6.)

(4)

And, passing by, he saw
the Scheme,
Of universal praise the
theme ;
Then went to BISH, a
Ticket bought,
In hopes that Fortune
he had caught.
(*Go to No.* 5.)

MOTHER GOOSE.

Though 'twixt my hooked nose and chin
I scarce can get my dinner in ;
Though deaf, half-blind, decrepid, bald,
And simple *Mother Goose* am call'd ;
Yet wit and worth refin'd, if poor,
Get but half the notice I procure.
And why ?—I'm rich. My *Goose,* to me,
Is worth a rich *State Lottery.*

Above: Cruikshank recycled his 1817 *Fortune's Ladder* - used on Bish posters - as a best-selling satire on George IV, who bribed the illustrator to drop his mockery.

Left: Another Cruikshank creation inspired by *Mother Goose*, the pantomime hit starring the immortal clown Grimaldi.

buzzing garden pests in *Dig For Victory*. Likewise, Cruikshank drew at least two designs for lottery puffs, Mother Goose (from the pantomime hit of the day starring the immortal clown Grimaldi) and a stereotyped pompous Queen, which were later reissued with different verses to market Robert Warren's shoe blacking. His famous advertisement for this product shows a cat fighting its own reflection in a polished boot, with the verse:

> Sudden I turn'd – beheld a scene
> I could not but delight in,
> For in my boot, so bright and clean,
> The cat her face was fighting

It made Warren's fortune and must be the first truly iconic advert.

The supremely talented illustrator led a chaotic life. He spent the evenings drinking in tobacco-wreathed low dives with other artists, journalists, actors, gamblers, and criminals, stumbling back late to his home where his irate mother pummelled him with her fists. Otherwise, he was 'pretty constantly in police custody during the early hours of the morning, having been found unconscious in the street,' according to the memoirs of his friend, the publisher Henry Vizetelly. This willingness to let himself go contrasted oddly with his personal vanity which caused him to 'stealthily eye himself in the glass on every opportunity,' according to Vizetelly, who revealed he would 'bring a long lock of scanty hair forward to try and conceal his baldness, and secure it in his place with an elastic band, which he foolishly hoped would be invisible to the most searching glances'. In later life he turned teetotal and, with the fanaticism of the convert, toured the country, lecturing forcefully on the evils of drink and rolling out graphic plates promoting temperance.

Yet like other artists notorious for their louche and disorderly personal lives (Francis Bacon springs to mind) Cruikshank was surprisingly disciplined when at work in the studio he shared with his elder brother Robert. Whatever the antics of the night before, and provided he was bailed from the watchhouse, he began sketching at nine o'clock precisely, filling in shadows with a watercolour wash until he was satisfied the drawing was sufficiently detailed to be sent to a wood engraver to be cut into a block. In this way, between 1810 and 1824, he made more than 360 separate designs used for lottery puffs. Most were for the Bishes, but other lottery contractors also commissioned him once they realised the value his quirky illustrations added to promotional handbills and posters. They vary in technical quality, since so much depended on the skill of the many different wood engravers, keepers of a mediaeval craft whose re-emergence coincided neatly with the new commercial age. Prints etched on expensive copper or steel plate required, however, a more complicated process, but print runs of 1,000 could be made from the former and 30,000 from the latter before sharpness was lost. In 1820, *The Observer* became the first newspaper to use prints; as a Sunday paper it had time to get the blocks engraved. Twelve years later the woodblock illustrated *Penny Magazine* appeared and was a great success. Despite *The Observer's* innovation, newspapers, which were too expensive for most people because of heavy taxes, rarely carried an illustration until 1842 with the arrival of the *Illustrated London News*, which Vizetelly helped to found. Cruikshank and dozens of other caricaturists sold their satirical and comical prints for 'sixpence plain, a shilling coloured' to mainly middle-class buyers, while the masses jostled and blocked pavements all over central London to gawk at them for free in the windows of scores of fiercely competing printshops. These picture galleries of current affairs at outlets like Knight's in Sweeting's Alley, Fairburn's off Ludgate Hill and Hone's in Fleet Street were so popular that the police on occasion had to disperse the crowds to keep thoroughfares open.

Cruikshank also set the scene for stock London characters of the Victorian era such as Sairy Gamp, a fat old drunken midwife with red nose and monstrously large bonnet who comically mangles the English language. She appears in Dickens' 1848 novel *Martin Chuzzlewit*, uttering gems like 'leave the bottle on the chimley-piece … but let me put my lips to it when I am so dispoged,' as she helps an undertaker prepare a body for burial. She was first created as part of a set of lottery puffs which Cruikshank mainly designed and were published in handbills and posters during January 1818 to promote a lucky draw for Twelfth Night, celebrated much more then than it is now. 'We understand that T. Bish, the Lottery Contractor, has exercised the ingenuity of various persons, in designing several sets of Twelfth-Night Characters,' observed the *Morning Chronicle*. Gamp, probably the most famous of these creations, is the perfect example of what the French poet Charles Baudelaire called his 'inexhaustible abundance of grotesque invention.' Another comic figure Cruikshank invented for Bish was Kitchen Maid, a surreal character made out of pots and pans and kitchen implements, which had great resonance as domestic servants played a major role in the economy, outnumbering manufacturing workers. (It is remarkably similar to figures which the French printmaker Nicholas de Larmessin created in 1680 for a series of copperplate engravings called *Les costumes grotesques*. These are clad in the objects that define their occupations, so that a blacksmith has horse shoe ears, for example.) Another grotesque in the same style was Greengrocer, almost certainly based on an extraordinary vegetable man, a life-sized model whose carrot arms boxed the clown Grimaldi on the pantomime stage and was said to have inspired Mary Shelley's *Frankenstein*. Instinctively, Bish knew such bizarre creations always grab the imagination and promote the product; the Michelin Man (tyres), orange Tango Man (soft drink), Mr. Cube (sugar), Potato Pete (wartime potatoes), drumming chimpanzees (milk chocolate), and talking meerkats (car insurance) are classic later examples. More conventional figures Cruikshank created for lottery ads included Sir William Wheedle, Sir Frederick Fidget, Miss Bounce, Lady Hemlock, Lucinda Lovely, Lucinda Lovesick, and Lady Penny Point. Often the illustrations were displayed in six cuts, almost like stage scenes in their theatrical presentation. This thespian treatment was to be expected from an actor manqué, soulmate of Edmund

KITCHEN-MAID.   COOK-MAID.

Mistress Molly, the Cook,
  At the Scheme only look,
In wealth we may both of
    us roll;
  If we *brush* for a prize,
  In the world we may
    rise,
And our *skuttles* have
  plenty of *Cole.*

If what you say's true,
  I'm all in a *stew,*
Lest we miss what we so
    much desire;
Should we lose this good
    plan,
  For a *sop in the pan,*
All the *fat* will be soon in
  the fire.

Left: Forerunner of the Michelin Man, Mr. Cube, Tango Man and many others. George Cruikshank created this surreal vegetable man to sell the lucky draws.

Above: More of Cruikshank's surreal figures.

GREEN-GROCER.

I am in the *basket;* but as I am a
medlar in the Lottery, a Prize may
give bad luck *turnips.* I hope to
cabbage a Capital; and in time to be
worth a *plum.*

Let's drink to Dame Fortune the bountiful lass,
Who gives us the pleasures that flow from the glass;
With cash in our pockets, a fig for Old Care,
And the wealth of the Lott'ry may all of us share!

NEW STATE LOTTERY CONTAINS

THREE of £30,000!

AND 6,711 OTHER PRIZES!

☞ *All Sterling Money!—No Stock Prizes!—No Classes!*
Every Ticket will be drawn singly!

£30,000 Money for the First Prize, First Day,

30th This Month,

(OCTOBER.)

NOT TWO BLANKS TO A PRIZE!

Tickets and Shares are selling by

T. BISH
STOCK-BROKER,
4, Cornhill, & 9, Charing-Cross,
LONDON,
And by all his Agents in the Country.

☞ BISH has sold more than Half of all the £30,000 Prizes
that have ever been; and in the last Lottery, Prizes of
£31,000, £20,000, £16,000, and Sixteen other Capitals!

. When there were THREE £30,000 Money Prizes in a former
Lottery, BISH SOLD THEM ALL!!!

Later handbills used Lowry-like matchstick men

Kean, possibly England's greatest ever tragedian, and unapologetic libertine, who visited the theatre and music hall as much as he could. One of Cruikshank's favourite haunts was the Sir Hugh Myddleton, the performers' pub opposite Sadler's Wells Theatre in north London. Figures from popular contemporary stage plays abounded; for some 1815 promotions Cruikshank used Mrs. Malaprop from Richard Sheridan's *The Rivals*, and Miss Hoyden and Lord Foppington from his *A Trip to Scarborough*, a long-forgotten Restoration drama which delighted modern audiences when Alan Ayckbourn updated it in 2007. Typical titles of these engaging series of drawings, designed to lure the unwary to part with their cash by playing on greed, were *The Way to Wealth, The Chances of Fortune, Fortune Favours the Brave, Fruits of Good Living, Luck's Progress, Prize in Sight, How to Get Up in the World* and *I'm not such a Goose to let it Pass Away*. Comical foreigners played their part; Baron von Donder-Dronk Smoke-Off from Germany, Don Fernando Whiskerando from Spain, Mohammed Stabdalla Bloodhoundo Ali Cut-Throato from Algiers and Sandy McBagpipe from Scotland. So did aristocratic figures, such as the King of Arms, Knight of the Thistle, The British Duchess and Knight of the Garter, along with archetypal characters such as Mr. Nobody, Sir Somebody, Lady Betty Nosey and Molly Clappertongue.

Much more original than the use of social, theatrical, literary and nursery tale stereotypes were visual innovations such as the Lowry-like matchstick men arranged like strip cartoons to tell a story and usually enlivened by amusing rhyming verses. They look surprisingly modern and cinematic. One, commissioned by Bish in 1824 and called *How to Grow Fat*, claims that by trying your luck you, too, can prosper and blossom out, like the little stick man in the picture who swells into a balloon. One figure says:

Tis BISH's house – I know
It well
The sequel I begin to smell

The other replies:

> You know his other in
> Cornhill? –
> Tis there you'll get a golden pill

Other witty dialogues between the stick men, who are sometimes shown as boxers under headings such as *Sport for the Fancy* [fight fans], invariably ring the changes on the eternal theme of how agreeable it would be to be rich. These early adverts, properly integrating copy and illustration for the first time and using new display faces, were a major breakthrough in mass communication. And Tom Bish can take the credit for this. Another innovation he introduced were the enigmatic pictorial puzzles and hieroglyphics which were printed on handbills and ornamental circulars, usually in red but often in stunningly embossed four colours. The answer to one of these enigmas (illustrator unknown) reads:

> If you are a man struggling through the world, or surrounded by crosses, or if you wish to lay a fortune for your children, go to BISH or his agents, who may make you independent, and above the frowns of the world.

This harked back to an earlier tradition, before house numbers came into being in the eighteenth century, when few could read and rebuses had to be puzzled out. These ornamental devices suggesting the name of the house owner might be two cocks for Cox or a hare and a bottle for Harebottle.

One visual Cruikshank stunt is his 1817 handbill headed 'PATENT SPECTACLES FOR THE NEW YEAR'. It consists of a giant pair of spectacles, like one of those adverts illustrated by the modern artist Peter Till who also surrealistically juxtaposes large and small objects. In one frame entitled *Before 21 January* (date of the draw) is a man facing famine, in the other entitled *After 21 January* is a man with a coach and horses and a £2,000 prize. Anti-lottery campaigners later adapted this device for their propaganda, putting in the frames a hanged woman ruined by lottery debts. Appropriately it was Cruikshank, as grand signor of the genre, who illustrated the final advertisements called *The Last of the Lotteries* published just before the old State Lottery was finally abolished in October 1826. They show a footman running and exclaiming:

Run, Neighbours, run the LOTTERY's expiring
When FORTUNE's merry wheel, it will never turn more

Another puff of his, called *Hubble, Bubble, Toil and Trouble*, shows a Bubble man saying:

But nothing has troubled me since I drew breath
Like the sudden approach of the LOTTERY's death

Practically every member of the Cruikshank family made money from advertising at one time or another. Isaac Cruikshank was an accomplished watercolourist, who exhibited at the Royal Academy, and also a political caricaturist. His prints, even-handedly mocking Napoleon as well as the British royal family and politicians like Charles James Fox, were compared to James Gillray and Thomas Rowlandson. To pay his bills, he designed and drew many lottery puffs between 1793 and 1800, although after that his output declined as his drinking increased. The Guildhall lotteries collection attributes to 'Sir Isaac Cruikshank' a number of ads commissioned by Goodluck, Richardson and other brokers in 1810, the year before he died from a drinking match. They include a charming series of line drawings, printed by James Whiting, called *Before and After St. Valentine's Day*, which shows scenes such as a woman leaving her needy, aged parents in Bristol for London and returning with a lottery prize. They are more likely to be by his first son, Robert, whose middle name was also Isaac, and who collaborated closely with brother George. That year seems to have been when he got into his stride with the depiction of characters like Captain MacHeath, King Arthur, Mrs. Brulgruddery and also Lady Africana Blackhall, complete with verse caption which sounds horrific to the modern and more enlightened reader:

See Africana with her sable face
Admit her freely to your Twelfth Night's pleasure
A dark complexion can be no disgrace
Where social virtues form an inward pleasure

A skilled draftsman, Robert, who was originally a midshipman on the East India Company's ship *Perseverance*, worked with his brother for many years. They illustrated the classic *Real Life in London* and returned constantly to the favourite theme of Napoleon caricatures. In one ad the exiled dictator is shown disconsolate on St. Helena underneath the caption:

Oh! Would they send, tho' not a slice of cake
A Lottery Prize 'twould then my fortune make

His final ad, headlined *A Prize in Sight*, seems to have been for the broker Sivewright for a draw on 12 April 1826, six months before abolition.

Another who took advertising commissions to make a living was Robert Seymour, who turned from professional oil painting with at least one work exhibited at the Royal Academy to commercial illustration. In doing so, he become a great comic artist. To promote a 12 April 1826 draw, he drew a splendid cartoon of Bish in jester's garb carrying a placard boasting, 'BISH has just sold two £30,000 and three £20,000 prizes All Within Three Months'. A month later, in another example of recycling, the lottery contractor Eyton, also based in Cornhill, used exactly the same image for one of his promotions, though obviously with a different placard. For a Hazard puff the same year, Seymour used the stick men motif in a series of drawings headed *Throw Physic to the Dogs. Dialogue between Mr. Thin and Mr. Stout.* Comic washerwomen were another favourite theme.

From this humble hackwork Seymour expanded to provide drawings for wood-engraved illustrations in children's stories, and for a wide range of books and periodicals, such as the satirical journal *Figaro in London,* forerunner to *Punch,* which he enlivened for years with humorous scenes before falling out with the editor in a vicious row. He also sold caricatures to printsellers, including Thomas McLean, who later started a caricature magazine called *Looking Glass.* Every month Seymour provided four large lithographed sheets of illustrations. He was a friend of George Cruikshank, working out with him at a gymnasium, though their relationship cooled when he began imitating George's style in caricatures under the pseudonym Short Shanks. Later, his series of lithographs, issued between 1834 and 1836, called *Sketches by Seymour,* portraying the comic adventures of lovable cockney sportsmen became best-sellers, and were reprinted for decades. He has even been credited as the true begetter of Charles Dickens' *The Pickwick Papers.* It is a tangled tale but seems to turn on his suggestion to the publisher Edward Chapman for a series of monthly sketches about a cockney sporting club. Chapman liked the idea and thought the twenty-three-year-old up-and-coming Dickens should write the accompanying text. The first instalment, called *The Posthumous Papers of the Pickwick Club,* was published. Then a power struggle began between writer and illustrator over who should control the project, Dickens insisting in a tense meeting that Mr. Pickwick should be drawn fat not thin. Before the second part appeared, on 20 April 1836, the highly strung and overworked Seymour shot himself in the head in his Islington summer house. Although some obituaries suggested the row had contributed to his untimely death at the age of thirty-eight, his suicide note to his wife Jane stated, 'blame, I charge you, no one'. He was not the only contemporary artist to succumb to the pressures of the job. Others included Luke Clennell, a distinguished wood engraver and pupil of the outstanding Northhumbrian wood engraver Thomas Bewick. Clennell was commissioned in 1814 to paint a huge picture of entertainment given to the Allied Sovereigns in Guildhall by a grateful City of London in order to celebrate the ending of the long Napoleonic wars. After three years working on this complicated project he became insane and was confined for years in a London lunatic asylum.

Another illustrator who died early, at the age of forty-eight in 1822 of overwork was the Yorkshireman John Thurston whose pen and pencil designs, often tinted with India ink, were brilliantly suitable for wood engraving. Although lacking Cruikshank's flair and fluidity, they made him for a while 'the principal artist in London who had any repute as a designer on the wood,' according to his contemporary Samuel Redgrave. Like so many of his colleagues, he exhibited at the Royal Academy, from 1794 to 1812, and was also an associate of the Society of Painters in Water Colours. He worked intermittently for the Bish company, producing for example twenty-four lottery puffs featuring dramatic characters for the 1814 Twelfth Night draw. His drawings are quirky and funny. They include Queen Dollalolla from *Tom Thumb*, Lady Sneerwell from *School for Scandal*, Archer from *Beaux Stratagem*, Romeo from *Romeo and Juliet*, Viola from *Twelfth Night*, and Miss Vixen Vinegar from *Provoked Spinster*. His main income, however, came from designing book illustrations; his work lit up most of the novels and volumes of poems published in the first two decades of the nineteenth century. Among them are the highly regarded *Religious Emblems* brought out by R. Ackermann in 1808 and the 1817 illustrated reprint of James Buckle's book *The Club*, originally published in 1711, which features twenty-four members ranging from Antiquary to Zany. Some of his drawings were engraved on copper, but most were cut on wooden blocks by expert craftsman such as Bewick with whom he collaborated on a number of publications.

Another creative partner was Robert Branston, a Norfolk man who engraved some of the outstanding figure drawings in *The Club*.

QUEEN DOLLALOLLA.

Give me, rogues, a glass of gin,
And put a little bitters in,
And give a glass to Mr. Noodle,
To drink a Prize to Mr. Doodle
Where's my royal husband too?
Do prythee call him—Doodle, do.
But if directly come he won't,
Then don't stay for him—Doodle, don't.

MISS VIXEN VINEGAR.

Not want of wit, or want of charms,
Has kept a husband from my arms ;
But all the men are grown so greedy,
They'll wed no maid, though fair—if needy.
But should I get a Lott'ry Prize,
I need not envy Cowslip's eyes,
For I'm in hopes of Mr. Noodle—
But if not him—I'm sure of Doodle.

Left: Queen Dollalolla from Tom Thumb promotes the 1814 Twelfth Night draw (artist John Thurston)

Right: Miss Vixen Vinegar from the play *Provoked Spinster*

Like George Cruikshank, he had been taught by his father, a general copperplate engraver and heraldic painter, and then moved to Bath, where he failed to get work. In 1799, at the age of twenty-one, he joined other novice engravers such as Bewick's pupil, Charlton Nesbitt, in trying his luck in rapidly expanding London where it was much easier to get employed. Initially, as did so many others, he supported himself by embellishing lottery bills with wood engravings before graduating to book illustrations. Here his forte was the precise and sensitive depiction of human subjects and not nature scenes where he could not compete with Bewick, whose genius outshone virtually everyone. He trained his son, also called Robert, along with other apprentices such as the brilliant fourteen-year-old John Thompson who was later to be hailed as 'the best English wood engraver of the present day'. Father and son worked together, churning out vast numbers of plates for books of all kinds and occasionally for commercial ads. Branston Junior seems to have been the shrewder businessman, forging partnerships with people like the printer Whiting, who had acquired Sir William Congreve's process for security printing in colours. This was a much more successful project than the dud Heath Robinson perpetual motion machine that Congreve had once invented. They created the firm Whiting and Branston, which specialised in banknotes and polychrome lottery advertising cards. These beautiful, high quality productions, which made their first appearance in 1820, are far superior to the usual poorly printed black and white giveaways. Surviving examples of the elaborately embossed three or four colour cards, which relied heavily on Congreve's compound-plate printing for their technical excellence, have a distinctive ceremonial feel, not unlike the invitation cards the firm supplied for George IV's coronation. Branston's brother Frederick also worked as an engraver for best-selling English and French publications, and later for magazines as did other family members throughout the nineteenth-century. The Branston clan made a huge and largely unacknowledged contribution to English picture printing.

Making commercial use of the vigorous creativity of Cruikshank, Lamb and other talented writers and illustrators required, however, another kind of talent. It needed a special kind of communications ability to organise the logistics of using their work to sell consumer products. The day of the advertising agency had arrived.

"Please don't tell my mum I work here –
she thinks I'm a doorman in a brothel"

CHAPTER SIX

The Admen

In 1786, for a one-shilling fee, entrepreneur William Tayler began to place advertisements for London businesses in the *Maidstone Journal*. He would have been amazed had he known he was sowing the seeds of an industry which today employs more than one million people worldwide (unquantifiable millions more if support and ancillary services are counted), creates commercial empires like Saatchi & Saatchi, so powerful they have tried to gobble up global banks, and bombards the average London commuter with 3,500 sales messages on a daily basis.

Many others soon followed Tayler in setting up as agents for the rapidly expanding provincial press to accept adverts, their commission paid by the newspaper proprietors. They were not creative advertisers but middlemen, who advised on suitable publications, ensured insertions were correctly placed and chased up payments. It was the Bishes, father then son (mainly the latter through his analytical and structured approach) who did so much to professionalise the work of these early pioneers, bringing precision and targeting to haphazard marketing. They were also able, gradually, to persuade conservative newspaper editors and proprietors to allow typographical and presentational innovations in the messy format of the 'puffs' published in their columns. Rarely was this easy. The *Morning Post* notoriously gave short shift to anyone trying to jazz up its dull layout with newfangled displays. Its ad manager was once so outraged by a suggestion that a certain announcement be set over two columns that he told the runner, 'Young man, go back and tell Mr. Jackson he should know better than to ask such a thing.' *The Times* also disliked its vertical lines being broken up by display advertisements, in contrast to weekly newspapers which were much more relaxed.

A turning point came with the realisation that it might be easier to sell space if the agent also offered to design the ad and write the copy on behalf of the client. Such a function lies at the heart of the modern advertising agency. This was the bright idea of a member of the Christ's Hospital mafia, lifelong chum of Charles Lamb and an eccentric who loved to dress up as Shakespeare's comic hero Falstaff: the exuberant and inimitable James 'Jem' White. He was to collaborate with Bish (Junior) in producing many imaginative ads whose style was eventually imitated by all other lottery brokers.

Academics have argued the pedantic toss whether it was White or Tayler (after he teamed up with a respectable Hereford man Thomas Newton in 1803 to form the firm Tayler and Newton) who was technically the first ad agent in the modern sense. The picture is blurred by the fact that the mechanics of commercial advertising were much less precise or specialised than they are now; everyone cheerfully joined in and functions overlapped, often chaotically. Not until the late nineteenth century did the idea of 'full service' advertising develop, with artists and copywriters employed full-time with neatly defined and discrete tasks. Later, media buyers, production executives and a whole host of other specialists appeared. On its website, the respected History of Advertising Trust, which holds the world's largest archive of UK advertising at Raveningham in the depths of the Norfolk countryside, states the R F White company is ' believed to be' the oldest UK agency. That is a fair verdict. The larger-than-life White employed copywriters like Charles Lamb on a freelance basis as early as the 1800s, advertised the Admiralty before Trafalgar and the War Office before Waterloo and for more than 130 years his firm kept the same account (the Sun Insurance Office Ltd), which must be an all-time record. As author of the *Original Letters of Sir John Falstaff and his Companions* which imitated Shakespeare, White was also a writer who might well have composed copy himself. His firm R F White & Son remained in the hands of his family until the death of his great-grandson Gilbert White in 1962, and existed as the recruitment advertising agency White, Bull Holmes Ltd until the late 1980s.

Jem's career as joker entrepreneur began at Christ's Hospital, which at this time was producing more celebrated writers – such as Coleridge and *Times* editor, Thomas Barnes – than any other school in the country. There, dressed as a dandy, though a 'Charity Boy', his wisecracks irritated the teachers but amused his school fellow Lamb, who later lamented, 'he carried away with him half the fun of the world when he died – of my world at least'. When he left school in 1790, White continued there as a clerk in the Counting House, starting an agency (first client Christ's Hospital) as a sideline ten years later in Warwick Square next door and moving to 33 Fleet Street in 1808. Other early clients were wine merchants, who settled in kind with brandy and port.

His friendship with Lamb deepened; they even lived together for a while, united by playfulness. They acted as waiters at the Smithfield feasts held annually in May for London chimney sweepers, merrily serving sausages with great gusto and singing songs standing on the trestle tables. It was 'a pleasure to see the sable younkers lick in the unctuous meat' wrote Lamb in his essay *In Praise of Chimney Sweeps*. The early feminist Elizabeth Montague, doyen of the Blue-Stocking Club, also entertained the 'younkers' in the grounds of her splendid Portman Square mansion at events which were much more magnificent, but less fun than those organised so chaotically by the comical duo. Other occasions where White liked to show off his sense of humour were the frequent dinner parties given by Lamb and his sister Mary, for the writer William Hazlitt, Leigh Hunt, editor of the crusading *Examiner* and other literary and journalistic figures; 'a numerous and odd set' but amusing company, recalled a frequent guest, Henry Crabb Robinson, diarist and the first modern war correspondent. Cracking jokes as he held court there or at his favourite haunt, the Feathers Inn in Hand Court, Holborn, where he sank huge quantities of Burton Ale, 'Sir John', as he was known to his friends, might have seemed conviviality writ large. But behind the clown's mask lay a ruthless businessman. In 1817, business was so good he was finally able to give up his Christ's Hospital job, buy a house with servants in Bloomsbury's fashionable Burton Crescent, and commission expensive miniatures of himself and his wife from royal miniature painter Sir William Newton; but that same year, James Savage, proprietor of a weekly newspaper the *Taunton and Bridgwater Journal and Western Advertiser*, owed him £100. White vindictively pursued Savage for this debt and put him in jail, to the great distress of Savage's family.

When he died after a short illness of unknown cause in 1820, James White was only forty-five years old. He left a thriving business to his widow Margaret, a bookseller's daughter, and their six children, and was the first to win fame and fortune from the ad industry. Many others were to follow him. The more diffident Thomas Newton, who also operated from Bloomsbury's long vanished Warwick Square, was not among them, although he managed to make a steady living. Unusually, among the notoriously rackety individuals then dominating the media, he was straight in business affairs. An 1825 obituary attributed his success to 'the correctness of his accompts [accounts] and the rectitude of his dealings, and enabled him, not withstanding a multitude of competitors, to bring up a large family in a most respectable way'. For this reason the Bishes trusted him implicitly, channelling through him for twenty years all their lottery ads for the provincial newspapers. Stock Exchange papers on a draw in 1809 lists a £243 13s 2d payment by Bish Senior for 'Country Ads'. Ten years later his son, in a textbook example of the meticulous way he always planned his campaigns, continued to relay through Newton the most precise instructions as to how his ads were to be placed.

On his behalf Newton sent a letter to newspapers from Aberdeen to Penzance enclosing two inserts puffing a particularly popular Lord Mayor's Day lottery held late in 1819, when lawyers, journeymen, diamond dealers, female servants and army captains all won major prizes. Each advertisement was headlined 'FIVE MINUTES WILL DECIDE £40,000' and started 'All drawn on 9 December. The two first prizes will each obtain £20,000 plus 4 other prizes of £20,000...' The letter read:

> SIR
>
> Please to insert the above as ordered, and I will thank you to display them as nearly as possible like the original [format], and it is MR. BISH's wish that his ADVERTISEMENTS may always be kept in a distinct column from any other Lottery advertisement, for when two or three are set together, they only form a confused mass.
>
> I am SIR & c
>
> Warwick Square, LONDON
>
> NOVEMBER 1819

Another letter insisted that a paragraph drawing attention to Bish's agents nationwide and their success in selling lottery tickets be inserted 'amongst the News in the same publication as the Advertisement'. This undisguised plug is an early example of an advertorial.

As well as advertising, Tayler and Newton also supplied news in the form of accounts of parliamentary proceedings, royal proclamations and speeches, stock exchange prices and snippets from foreign gazettes. The service was, however, limited and confined to the provinces, with only one London evening newspaper supplied. A rival company set up in 1812 by Charles Barker and a *Times* printer called James Lawson also handled City, parliamentary and overseas news, as well as placing ads in *The Times*. Thomas Alsager, the paper's famous business correspondent, worked out of its offices at 12 Birchin Lane from 1817. But the ambitions of Lawson & Barker went much further and explains why it soared ahead of companies like Streets and Deacons, which also brokered advertising space, to become the internationally renowned firm of Charles Barker and Sons, oldest advertising agency in the city of London. It survived until 2009 as BNB Recruitment Solutions.

In the 1820s it was already displaying the flair which, with the financial backing of the merchant banker Nathan Mayer Rothschild, made it so pre-eminent in promoting banks and other financial institutions as well as start-ups, particularly new railway companies during the 1840s railway mania. One innovation was a daily newsletter for clients, standard practice for agencies today who now mainly send copies electronically. Then, underpaid clerks had laboriously to copy the information by hand and dispatch via the General Post Office at Lombard Street to recipients who ranged widely from a Swansea newspaperman called Jenkins to the Prussian Consul-General Mr. Bourcard of 31 Broad Street Buildings. The newsletter summarised the hourly reports made to the agency of every transaction on the London and foreign Stock Exchanges, latest newspaper reports worldwide, and commercial and political intelligence furnished by 'merchants of the first respectability'. One still survives, written in clear copperplate, dated 5 March 1824. A typical entry read:

> Govt has received despatches from Sir W. A'Court of Madrid dated 24th ult stating that great efforts were making (sic) to remove the existing Ministry and that a petition for that purpose, signed by 2,000 of the inhabitants of Madrid, had been presented to the King.

Another item said it regretted:

No expresses have arrived today from France which is to be entirely attributed to the state of the weather, the vessels not being able to leave Calais harbour.

A major task of the agents was to negotiate with the newspapers on advertising rates for their clients. In the early days they appear to have been fixed, with little scope for flexibility. The Rev. Dr. Trusler's *London Adviser and Guide* gives some indication of the rates demanded in 1790 by the *Daily Advertiser*, *Gazetteer*, and *Ledger*, mainly circulating in the City of London, and the *Morning Post*, *Morning Chronicle* and *Herald*, mainly circulating in 'the west end of the town, among the gentry'. It states 'Ads in front of morning papers are inserted if not above 18 lines in length, for 5s 6d, in other parts of the paper for 3s 6d. In the evening papers the price is 4s each time. Price increases with length, about a penny or three halfpence a line. Out of every ad, Govt has 2s 6d. Ads in Gazette [Government paper], however short, is 10s 6d.' As ever, the government had its pound of flesh; its 2s 6d tax was later raised by a shilling and a 4d stamp was required for each newspaper, a heavy charge which was cut to a penny only in 1836.

By 1810, as newspapers began employing advertisement clerks such as the bookseller George Street hired by *The Times*, the business became much more sophisticated and commercial. Deals were offered with all kinds of rates on the table, the agent bargaining with the paper and getting his space for as little as possible, pocketing what he saved on the price. The rate card meant nothing, as is the case today. The price quoted might be 6d an inch, the contract eventually placed 3d an inch. Generally, the London papers were more likely to adhere to the printed rates while the remoter provincial papers accepted virtually anything; a West of Ireland periodical used to take halfpenny an inch for a six-inch double column advertisement. When Bish helped launch the 1822 fund-raising campaign on behalf of the London Committee for the Relief of the Distressed Irish, the cost of their announcements ranged from £11 11s for 291 lines in *The Times* to just £2 8s for 180 lines in the evening *Sun*. A year later the Lawson & Barker agency recorded these rates for advertisements it placed in the *Morning Chronicle* published on 8 September 1823:

Eight Lines (in Nonpareil Type) Seven Shillings
All above Eight Lines Sixpence each Line
Paragraph One shilling each Line
Servants wanting places Five shillings each
Births, Marriages, Deaths. Half a guinea each

These charges seem to have been reasonable, making newspapers relatively cheap for advertising, although stamp duty made them expensive to buy, and put them beyond the reach of the working classes.

As with the Internet today circulation figures were vague, if they were disclosed at all. 'This paper is very extensive in its circulation and is received in all fashionable circles,' declared the conservative *Morning Post* grandly and rather inaccurately in 1790. When Daniel Stuart and his brother Peter bought it five years later for a few hundred pounds it was selling barely 350 copies a day. Only slowly did its circulation increase to 7,000 when it was sold for £25,000 due to increasing profits made on the advertising boom. The commercial pressures of duty being charged at the same rate on each insertion regardless of length encouraged long boring advertisements since the longer the notices the less duty there was to pay. Gradually this reactionary approach changed as competition intensified during the rapid media expansion of the first quarter of the nineteenth-century. To win and retain readers the newspaper proprietors, including provincial owners who proved to be surprisingly creative and adaptable, became on the whole more receptive to fresh presentational methods. Bish and the ad agents continued to force the pace, making many suggestions which were acted upon.

They embraced the commonsense ideas, so obvious to us today, that publishing many miscellaneous adverts attracts more buyers, and that jumbled up adverts made the page look unattractive and clumsy; gradually these were sorted into categories like book advertisements, sales by auction, lotteries, servants, properties and medicines. The new look worked. Lord Milton wrote to his father from Naples in 1818 how much he missed the entertaining British press. 'We laugh at the tittle-tattle of the newspapers, at the advertisements for the lottery, patent blacking & c,' he wrote, 'but if the newspapers were deprived of all this nonsense and reduced to the paragraphs which announce great public events, they would go a very little way towards presenting their readers with an idea of the English world and the incessant motion and activity it is distinguished from others'.

As well as jazzing up newspapers, the innovators experimented with a variety of new methods including putting ads on the back of playbills to target theatre audiences, inserting loose flyers inside newspapers or binding them in magazines, and developing a primitive form of advertising mail. Bish kept a list of lottery ticket customers and prospective customers and regularly sent them, via speedy mail coaches, enticing one-page printed promotions about forthcoming draws. This was one of the first uses of junk mail which today in Britain has expanded into a hugely profitable business which generates £16 billion in sales each year. One typical missive, dated December 1824, was sent from his 'State Lottery Offices' at 4 Cornhill and 9 Charing Cross, London, to the Cobb family described as bankers of Margate. With its bold sub-headings, intelligent spacing and seductive prose, it is attractively presented and easy to read. In the time-honoured tradition of marketing ploys, the circular offers an incentive. Anyone buying a ticket before the first draw on 16 December is assured, under 'a very advantageous mode of adventure', of getting back most of their money if their ticket wins only a small prize or is undrawn from the lottery wheel. Under this cashback arrangement a ticket priced at £22 19s 0d actually costs only £4 19 0d (£18 0 0 being returned). Its divisions are similarly discounted, so that a sixteenth of a ticket priced at £1 12s 0d, favourite purchase of domestic servants, costs only 9s 6d (£1 2s 6d being returned). Jackpots of £30,000 and £20,000 are offered, a huge amount of money then, along with lucky numbers that had won major prizes before. Dozens are listed in black lettering 'reserved for my country friends'. Haste is advised to prevent disappointment 'as the Sales are unprecedentedly great'. Bish stresses it is 'needless' to mention how often his tickets win prizes, but then goes on to do precisely that, boasting 'I sold Three £30,000 all in One Lottery, an event unprecedented in Lottery annals.' The sign-off, 'Your much obliged humble Servant, T. BISH stock-broker,' prints his name in the largest type on the page, and is clearly designed to reinforce the brand. Curiously though, he seems to have missed a trick with the envelope, which has only a handwritten address on it and no printed logo. Perhaps the postal system before the days of the penny post simply did not allow for pre-printed envelopes. On hand-delivered circulars, the equivalent of direct mail, it was possible to signpost attached offers. One Bish example, headed 'THE PUBLIC'S OWN LOTTERY', even has a verse and starts:

To the Lady or Gentleman
With the Compliments of the Season
T. BISH the Contractor, respectfully
Presents the Inclosed
New Year's Lottery begins 21 January (1817)

Flyers were also distributed with newspapers, though it is unclear whether the advertisers organised this themselves or through agents. A trade association, the Society of Dealers in Newspapers, assiduously promoted this facility. An advert in 1817 promised '8,000 handbills in morning newspapers to London and suburbs within a few hours, 17,000 on a Sunday morning. Each bill read by 3 people'. The cost was a reasonable £1 16s 0d for each week day delivery, £2 12s 0d for Sunday. Another effective distribution method, which Bish started, was 'piggy-backing', whereby a promotional leaflet was pasted onto the outside back cover of a periodical or sown inside it with a binding on the left-hand edge so it could be torn off. Surprisingly this simple device, now used everywhere, was not taken up again in any major way until much later in the nineteenth century.

Theatre audiences were long accustomed to adverts on the back of their cast lists. One given out at the Theatre Royal, Drury Lane in 1818 begins, 'While you are waiting for the Performance to begin, Permit me to direct your attention to a subject of much Importance – the means of acquiring an Independence.' Then followed the inevitable lottery puff. Nor did circus audiences escape. Everyone attending Hull's 'Olympic Circus' on Monday 14 October 1822 was given a raffle ticket with the prize of a sixteenth share of a ticket in the state lottery drawing at the end of the month. Racegoers crowding into the Chester Races in May that year found blazoned on their programmes the news that 'by order of Mr. Bish' the jockey winning the Tradesman's Cup race would be presented with an eighth share of a lottery ticket. 'The constant success of Mr. BISH's extraordinary good luck,' it was suggested, 'may cause the Rider to be the greatest Winner'. These brash marketing methods which relied on repetitive messages were effective and laid the foundations for selling by way of 'brands' The most ingenious – and controversial – invention, however, was outdoor advertising.

CHAPTER SEVEN

Battle of the Billboards

Commercial images bombard us constantly – from subterranean tube escalators, right up to the sky. Newspapers, magazines, freesheets, radio, television, internet, mobile phones, awnings, sides of buildings, toilets, rubbish bins, health centres, supermarkets, airports, buses, taxis, boats, trains and planes (the list is endless), are all ingeniously and creatively enlisted so that the entire landscape seems to project in-your-face advertising. Unless you live in the Brazilian metropolis of Sao Paolo, which has boldly banned all outdoor advertising, there is no escape. Experiments have shown that during a forty-five-minute journey the average London commuter is exposed to more than 130 sales messages, featuring some eighty different products. Over a day, this figure rises to a staggering 3,500. Advertising seizes on new communication technologies as soon as they are developed and, abhorring a vacuum, always expands to fill whatever space is available. It was ever thus.

Of course it would be absurd to claim that Tom Bish single-handedly invented the art of outdoor advertising. Booksellers, auctioneers, circus owners and patent medicine salesmen also helped to develop the medium in the early nineteenth century, painting advertising messages on rocks and fences and sticking up bills. Yet it is a fair deduction, from the evidence of contemporary notes, that he took the lead in using it systematically as part of a wider marketing strategy, in a way that modern admen would readily recognise and appreciate. Broadsides in particular, pasted up or handed out, complemented his other promotional tools.

The nuisance of distributors blocking pavements as they thrust giveaways at passers-by outside tube stations is as nothing compared to the way advertising blighted the streets two hundred years ago. Horse-drawn giant top hats, enormous tea caddies and Brobdingnagian Wellington boots paraded along Oxford Street, swerving into people and being 'a perfect nuisance', according to *Punch*. It complained, 'Go where you will, you are trapped by a monster cart running over with advertisements, or are nearly knocked down by an advertising house put upon wheels.' These ungainly advertising carts fascinated foreign visitors to London during the 1820s. The German garden designer, Prince Hermann Pückler-Muskau, compared them to grounded Noah's Arks plastered with posters, voyaging ponderously through the streets 'carrying more lies upon them than Munchausen ever invented'. Men with placards on poles also obstructed the roads and were shooed away by the beadles who also had to deal with residents' complaints about horns being blown late at night to support of one promotion or another.

Apart from advertising carts, print shop windows and newspapers which the gentry mainly bought, the main means of mass communication were posters, handbills and billboards. Hundreds of thousands of literate consumers, who could not afford a daily paper, could be targeted this way. Another huge advantage was that there was no tax on them. In London, expert bill-stickers, capable of putting up 400 bills a day, plastered advertisements everywhere from suburban garden fences to the rugged sides of four-storey buildings. These they covered with enormous sheets, neatly and astonishingly precisely using an instrument like an elongated fishing rod with a cross staff at the end known as a 'peel'. Somehow they even managed to stick gigantic posters, sometimes as large as thirty-six sheets, under the arches of

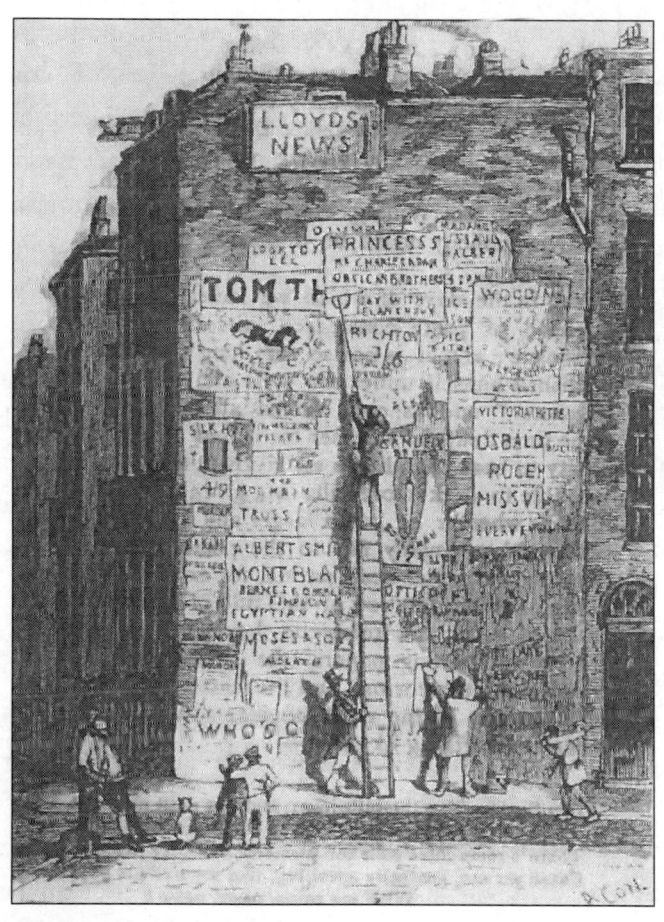

Above: Bill-stickers at work. Charles Dickens admired their ingenuity

Left: Mr. Perry's mobile advertisement was a familiar sight along London's crowded Regent Street in the 1830s

the bridges over the Thames. They ignored the numerous BILL-STICKERS BEWARE notices, which themselves of course only worsened the environmental pollution. They also cheerfully ignored the desperate attempts by Parliament to control the nuisance such as the 1817 Metropolitan Paving Act, which ordered that hoardings must not be erected without a licence from the local Surveyor of Pavements. In 1820, the Home Secretary George Canning personally ordered heavy-handed raids on premises throughout London which resulted in the arrest of scores of bill-stickers and the seizure of hundreds of their placards. He was mocked and lampooned in the popular press. Rows with householders were frequent. On one occasion a tradesman called Powell, finding a man posting walls on the side of his house, beat him violently with the peel and was charged with assault. The magistrate, one Curling, was however entirely sympathetic, threatening the bill-sticker in court, 'if you ever come to my house in that way I will break every bone in your skin.'

Author and illustrator Alfred Forester, complaining of bill-stickers in 1834, wrote 'there is scarcely a brick or a board in city or suburb, however newly erected, in highway or byway but is speedily adorned by their handiwork'. Later, the chronicler of the early Stock Exchange, John Francis recalled, 'Puffs, paragraphs and papers circulated wherever the ingenuity of man could contrive, the public thoroughfares were blazoned by day and lighted by night with advertisements.' Even Samuel Coleridge, his poetic sensibilities offended perhaps, was moved to comment on the blight. In a 1826 letter to his friend, James Gillman Junior, he refers to the nationwide advertising campaign in support of the last ever lottery draw. 'Mr. Bish mourns [the last draw], in large Capitals, red, blue and black, in every corner.' Nearly twenty-five years later Blackwood's *Edinburgh Magazine* remembered this campaign with a shudder. 'The image of the vans, placards, and handbills of Bish,' it declared, 'is still fresh in our memory and we pray devoutly that succeeding generations may never behold a similar mistake'. This prayer was never answered. Early in Queen Victoria's reign outdoor advertising took off. Posters promoting theatres, auctions, books, patent medicines, drinks, clothes, and shoe polish were slapped on virtually every hoarding around the many building sites of the burgeoning capital, on boarded fences at Waterloo Bridge, steamboat piers, walls besides the English Opera House in North Wellington Street, condemned houses in Newport Street, the enclosure around Nelson's Column in Trafalgar Square, the Royal Exchange, and even the Fleet Prison. They were crude and totally lacking in subtlety. A Victorian Andy Warhol would have had difficulty in transmuting these lurid images of consumer culture into pop art. Compared to 'that mincing elaborateness of finish' of engravings in print shop windows, wrote a 1843 commentator, 'they have all the boldness, if not much of the imagination and artistical skill of Salvator Rosa, and may compete the palm in roughness at least, with the Elgin Marbles in their present weather-worn condition'. He added their 'colossal specimens of typography' made book pages look like 'a snug citizen's box placed besides the pyramids of Egypt'. Gigantic pens were held by huge hands, enormous spectacles 'fit to grace the eyes of an ogre', and a domestic drama 'in the shape of one man shooting another on the quarter-deck of a vessel in flames, off the coast of Van Diemen's land, with emigrants and convicts of all shapes and sizes crowded on the shore'. Another drama, at the Queen's Theatre, featured a view of the Khyber Pass with Lady Sale, heroine of the First Afghan War, at the top of it brandishing a pistol in either hand 'beneath the cocked and leveled terrors of which a row of turbaned Orientals kneel on either side'.

Outside London, bill-stickers carrying ladders, pails of whitewash and big brushes had no qualms about desecrating the countryside, angering householders from Cornwall to Ross and Cromarty by their skill in covering the high walls of rural gardens with huge ads in a single night. According to a contemporary account this often happened 'while the old charlies or watchmen were asleep in their roadside boxes, from whence they issued to call the hour, and give timely notice to bill stickers and burglars to conceal themselves'. In Exeter, the autumn Mayor's Court in 1826 condemned 'the unseemly practice that has of late prevailed of covering the trees on Northernhay [a park] with printed bills, to the great annoyance of valetudinarians, whose eyes, instead of being relieved by the lovely verdure they were wont to look upon, now at every turn encounter Morris Jacobs' cheap clothes, the last sighings of Bish, Sivewright, Swift etc'. It promised to clear away the unsightly posters so that the walk will 'once again become a delightful promenade for citizens and strangers'.

As one of the major perpetuators of this vandalism, Bish sent his provincial bill-stickers known as 'trampers' to every town and city in Britain where they worked for up to six months at a time. A stickler for detail, he was remarkably precise as to their duties. This is evident in a template of his orders to them headed 'INSTRUCTIONS for the Station Men on their routes to their headquarters' (for a series of lottery draws starting on 21 January 1817). It begins:

> You are to proceed on the outside of the Coach [it was cheaper than inside] to BLANK taking with you your PASTE-pan, Pad, Claw and other Appurtenances. If there are any agents in the Town call on them as soon as you can after your arrival, deliver Mr. Bish's letter and enquire if they have any Bills they wish stuck.

He further instructed that in addition handbills were to be given at 'Gentlemen's Houses, Inns, Public Houses, Barbers' Shops, Blacksmiths etc and small cards for Public Houses, Bakers' and Barbers' shops.' Finally, they were told, 'Write every Sunday and Wednesday giving particulars of what you have done.'

But if the Bishes tightly controlled their itinerant toilers at the promotional coal-face, they were also loyal to them. During the 1809 Old Price Riots at Covent Garden, young James Andrews was arrested for distributing handbills outside the theatre attacking the management. Immediately, Bish Senior leapt to his defence, writing newspaper letters claiming the attack was justified and standing bail for him. At Bow Street Magistrates Court Andrews explained he had done nothing wrong as 'he got his bread by distributing bills, having for 15 months been engaged by Mr. Bish who would give him a character'. Eleven years later Bish Junior successfully fought off a proposed draconian law which sought to empower 'any person whatever, with or without a warrant, to seize and take away any bill-sticker'. Magistrates would then have been allowed 'to commit such a person to the house of correction' for between seven and fourteen days.

Inside the capital, the Bishes was equally well organised. One report headed 'An Account of the Situations where Mr. Bish's boards are placed' lists their locations in great detail from 'Mr. Gilding Butcher near Stratford Turnpike' to 'Mr. Brown Fishmonger Knightsbridge'.

He did not always get his own way, though. An attempt to put up a billboard in Palace Yard by the old House of Commons at Westminster failed, 'the streetkeeper not permitting it, it was fetched away and carried to Mr. Bish's Office, Charing Cross'.

Possibly the greatest innovation in outdoor advertising came in 1815 when Bish Junior sold all three £30,000 prizes in the April lucky draw. Despite competitors' claims that Irish lottery contractors had sold two of the winning tickets, he capitalised upon this spectacular event 'unparalleled in the history of lotteries' by placing large adverts in all national and regional papers. Then he pulled his masterstroke, with the forerunner of the neon lights that would later illuminate public spaces from Piccadilly Circus to Times Square. City workers pushing home along crammed Charing Cross and Cornhill were amazed and delighted one evening to see the entire fronts of his offices in both streets covered with Chinese lanterns shining out the message:

All THREE 30,000l Prizes were shared and sold by BISH

'BISH's offices were most brilliantly illuminated last night in consequence of his extraordinary luck in the Lottery just finished,' said the *Morning Chronicle* of 21 April. Exactly six years later, in a story headlined ANNIVERSARY OF LUCK the same newspaper reported that the letters were still there and that 'large purchases [of tickets] are always made at his offices on the anniversary of that day'.

The bill-stickers slogged away at more pedestrian work. These familiar street figures, wearing fustian jackets with huge pockets, carrying brown Holland bags and festooned with tin paste-boxes, became folk heroes, their exploits celebrated on stage, in prose and in verse. One anonymous 1830s ballad began:

> I'm Sammy Slap, the bill-sticker, and you must all Agree, Sirs,
> I sticks to bus'ness like a trump and Bus'ness sticks to me, sirs

In their own way, these 'knights of the brush', were regarded as artists. Some even had their own individualised stationery. Where to stick bills requires 'intellect as well as taste' said one commentator, who claimed 'the profession is as nearly as possible on a level with the Hanging Committee of the Royal Academy; and the spirit that animates the two bodies seems as similar as their occupations.' That may be stretching it a little, but they certainly had many admirers. Among them was Dickens who, predictably, gives the most graphic account of their peripatetic and colourful way of life in an highly entertaining essay called 'King of the Billstickers'. Perhaps he had a soft spot for them; over the years they plastered thousands of broadside announcements of his forthcoming books on hoardings everywhere. The essay, published in an 1851 issue of his magazine *Household Words*, describes the impact of their work and speaks of 'an old warehouse which rotting paste and rotting paper had brought down to the condition of an old cheese … it was so thickly encrusted with fragments of bills that no ship's heel after a long voyage could be half so foul'. The self-styled King, who claimed to have invented the advertising cart, said he was son of the 'Engineer, Beadle and Bill-Sticker to the parish of St. Andrew's Holborn' in the 1780s, and carried on the tradition. In an interesting side-light on the boom in State lotteries, he revealed that far fewer women were employed to stick up posters as the printers such as Evans and Ruffy of Walbrook, Thoroughgood and Whiting of The Strand, Gye and Balne of Gracechurch Street, began to produce much larger, and heavier, bills. And during the boom the male bill-stickers would not allow anyone to wilfully cover or destroy their bills as they had 'a society among themselves and very frequently dined together at some public house where they used to go of an evening to have their work delivered'. That changed with the abolition of lotteries. 'All that good feeling has gone,' he explained, 'nothing but jealousy exists, through the rivalry of each other … they were always employing a lot of ruffians from the Seven Dials to come and fight us … fighting scenes took place that beggars description.' The King concluded with words of wisdom that still apply today: 'You could hardly put too little in a poster; what you wanted, was, two or three good catch-lines for the eye to rest on – then, leave it alone – and there you were!'

Gradually the vicious pitched battles between rival gangs for the best positions abated as, very slowly, the industry became regulated. The Metropolitan Police Act 1839, forerunner of a whole raft of later legislation, made it an offence to put up posters without consent on any building, wall fence or poll. From the 1860s rented and protected 'Stations of External Paper-Hangers' started to spread in London and the major cities following an experiment in Leeds. About this time the first leased hoarding appeared in America along the fence surrounding the site where the New York City Post Office was being built. Various clubs and associations were formed which turned the trade into a respectable profession by keeping on the right side of the law and setting standards and establishing codes of practice. They did not always found favour. One of the earliest bodies seeking to regulate the trade was the Effectual Reform Bill-Sticking Association which made a modest start in 1840 by hiring a huge board in Billingsgate and charging its members four shillings a week to use it. A freelance bill-sticker 'of the ancient school' called John Davey began sticking up bills without permission and was summoned. In court he defended himself robustly and elegantly, arguing the association was a monopolistic novelty bent on taking money 'out of the pockets of the old right sort of bill-stickers, whose fathers and grandfathers and great grandfathers had been all their lives teaching the walls to speak to the public'. Amid laughter, he added the association was notorious for 'introducing all the most rascally quacks of all trades to the citizens of London'. He won the case. Today there is strict control. You cannot slap up an ad wherever you like. This does not deter fly-posters; eight out of ten UK local councils have a problem, mainly with local groups puffing concerts and political events but occasionally, and surprisingly, with well-known international companies who contract local ad agencies for fly-posting to cover their tracks. Several have been threatened with anti-social behaviour orders. There have also been cases of councils themselves doing deals with advertisers to use bus stops, benches and street lamps for promotions. This is a throwback to the 1860s when the West End theatre Adelphi promoted *The Dead Heart* by sticking ten million heart-shaped labels on everything in London from the Old Bailey to glasses in public houses. The US is more open, even boasting a website dedicated to the promotional flyer 'community' which, it claims, provide 'a true form of American pop art'.

Fears that the increase in cable television channels, dramatic rise in internet use with its dinky, irritating, pop-up ads, and increasingly sophisticated mobile phone devices will threaten outdoor advertising have proved totally unfounded. It is booming, greatly aided by digitalisation which produces computer-painted vinyl bulletins. At the height of the UK recession in 2009, revenues from outdoor ads using this new technology grew compared to newspaper, television and radio ad sales which all fell. In 2010, spending totalled £880 million. There is no mystery about this success story. Digital billboards can be changed at the touch of a button, allowing precise targeting of audiences, such as the hundreds of flat-screen TVs all round Heathrow's Terminal 5 showing ads which change day and night according to the flights selected.

They also draw the viewer in a way that static outdoor formats cannot; twice as many people look at these digital bulletins than traditional posters, and for around sixty per cent longer, according to research. Rapid digitalisation also means greater interactivity, with consumers increasingly able to buy a product by pointing their mobile phone at an ad. Old-fashioned billboards can, however, hold their own with a simple visual idea creatively executed. Over the years, there have been brilliant examples from British Airways, *The Economist*, the *Financial Times*, Heinz, and Marmite, among others. Outdoor advertising in unconventional places is also effective. Bish realized this back in 1826 when, in an early example of guerilla marketing, he created a buzz in the streets by employing choristers to shout out songs about the demise of lotteries as they marched along. One began:

Oh dear! What can the matter be?
To tell, who can be at a loss?
The people are running by hundreds to Bish's
To make out their dreams, and fulfil all their wishes,
To try and come in for the loaves and the fishes,
At Cornhill number 4, and 9 Charing Cross

Other performers recited funeral speeches to the crowds about the ending of the lucky draw. Rival brokers imitated his unusual campaign to target consumers. Such antics are now commonplace. Witness the highly successful 2009 stunt when hundreds of flashmob dancers, mimicking an advert for the T-Mobile phone company in a carefully choreographed sequence, temporarily closed Liverpool Street station. The hilarious footage became an instant YouTube hit and has been widely broadcast since. Another clever example of street publicity was Hewlett Packard and the National Gallery's 2007 Grand Tour of the streets of Soho and Covent Garden when they 'set free' masterpieces from the National Gallery. During a three-month period Londoners were treated to the sight of the moving works, reproduced by HP printers from paintings by artists such as Caravaggio and Titian. A wonderful example of a static site was the mineral water company Evian's sponsorship of Brockwell Lido in south London, which was threatened with closure. It spent £100,000 on essential repairs and painted a giant Evian logo on the bottom of the pool – located directly below a Heathrow flight path. The London Eye, which dominates the city's skyline, has also served as a monster billboard. The most entertaining, and much quoted, example of outdoor advertising has to be the enormous image of television personality Gail Porter's bare posterior projected on to the side of the Houses of Parliament in 1999 to promote the men's magazine *FHM*. More than forty million people are said to have seen the resulting news picture through the mainstream media. The Porter coup is likely to be exceeded only by Pepsi's plan to project its logo on the surface of the moon. This has not happened yet, but who knows?

Some advertisers claim their brands can enhance the environment in more tasteful ways, such as the ingenious temporary greening of Trafalgar Square in support of a campaign for Visit London, the body that promotes tourism to the capital. Yet environmental pollution is as divisive an issue as it was two hundred years ago, notably in America, the first nation on wheels. 'The highway has become the buyway,' declared a 1923 advertisement for the Outdoor Advertising Agency of America. 'It is millions of miles long. And billions of dollars are spent because of what the public sees when it travels this buyway … outdoor advertising pays and pays and pays.' The aesthetic, moral and legal issues of projecting commercial messages across public space from private property provoked a bitter fight which is unlikely ever to be resolved. In one corner were the advertisers self-servingly claiming the billboards as a colourful expression of the American way of life, in the other were concerned and environmentally conscious citizens, mainly women, dubbed dismissively 'the scenic sisters'. They have won round some surprising supporters. 'As a private person, I have a passion for landscape, and I have never seen one improved by a billboard,' confessed David Ogilvy, founder of the Ogilvy & Mather advertising agency, in his 1963 memoirs. Using public highways to promote products by targeting drivers and their passengers causes the same controversy in Britain. Hammersmith and Fulham Council took media owner Clear Channel to court after residents complained that the company's digital billboards on London's Fulham Palace Road blighted the area and could cause car accidents. In Notting Hill, David Cameron objected to them dominating his neighbourhood and projecting huge electronic adverts into the night. Elaborate poster sites on the road from London to Heathrow airport, inventive and creative as they may be, are not universally popular. The Green Party particularly has campaigned hard against the whole landscape being turned into one moving commercial image. No-one knows how advances in technology will transform outdoor advertising by the twenty-second century. But it is likely that sky, air and space itself, in ways as yet undreamt of, will all be used to promote consumer messages. Bish would be proud.

Yet even as he was inventing new ways of selling, the ingenious entrepreneur became increasingly concerned at the thought of the State lottery ending in 1826, depriving him of a major source of income. He looked for another money-making opportunity and found it in relaunching a national institution that has been immortalised in novels from Henry Fielding to Charles Dickens, patronised by monarchs from Charles II to Victoria and every social class from aristocrats to domestic servants, and acclaimed in its time as one of the wonders of the world: the celebrated Vauxhall Pleasure Gardens.

Rebranding works for some people

CHAPTER EIGHT

Rebranding Works

Save for a rather drab commemorative display board put up by the local council and a couple of artificial-looking grass tumps (probably the launching pads for the spectacular midnight firework displays that so annoyed local people), for years little remained of the fairyland that was Vauxhall. Yet its groves, grottos, covered arcades and temples, beautifully lit with tens of thousands of Chinese lanterns, had enchanted generations of Londoners from the Restoration onwards. This much-loved democratic pleasure garden, sited just across the River Thames from where Tate Britain is now, vanished without trace. When it was finally closed in 1859, property developers built over the site which re-emerged, courtesy of Hitler's bombers, as a small public park off Kennington Lane called Spring Gardens. A part has become Vauxhall City Farm. Some of the original spirit survived in nearby Bonnington Square where, despite bureaucratic interference, residents lovingly maintained in homage a tiny magical grove of lush sub-tropical plants, vines, trees and sculptures strung with fairy lights.

But in 2012, an imaginative makeover organised by local residents through the Friends of Vauxhall Pleasure Gardens, working with Lambeth Borough Council and neighbouring architects DSDHA, restored the park to some of its former glory. A glowing new entrance appeared on Kennington Lane next to the Royal Vauxhall Tavern, famous for its gay cabaret nights, so in keeping with the spirit of the pleasure garden's louche past. Two eighteen-metre-high black concrete cylindrical columns, sculptures in their own right with sensual curves, light up at night in various colours to welcome visitors. New landscaping, plantings and all-weather sports pitches for local youngsters grace this once seedy, dilapidated area which has been renamed with its original title of Vauxhall Pleasure Gardens. The Queen Anne Bar on the north side of the park, which featured exotic dancers as its main attraction, is now the Tea House Theatre, wonderfully done up in Victorian style. Appropriately, the celebrity who opened the renovation was comedian Paul O'Grady, otherwise known as Lily Savage, who began his career performing in the Vauxhall Tavern in the 1980s.

Back in 1821, though a contemporary London guide book promised 'the effect upon first entering baffles all description' the gardens, which opened during the summer on Mondays, Wednesdays and Fridays at 7 p.m, were beginning to lose their lustre. Their eighteenth-century heyday under Jonathan Tyers, proprietor and arts lover, who with his son built up the site into a fashionable evening venue, applauded by Dr. Johnson as 'that excellent place of entertainment peculiarly adapted to the tastes of the English nation,' had long gone. Takings were down, partly due to the recession following the ending of the Napoleonic wars, and partly because the attractions had become stale and the promenading passé. One newspaper complained of 'the monotony of marching round and round the same walks, perpetually molested by the same places. ... In the intervals all is dreariness'. There was evidently a limit to the times you could listen to the scrapings of out of tune fiddlers wearing cocked hats or to the warblings of the resident singer murdering popular songs of the kind Theodore Hook parodied so brilliantly at the pianoforte.

Visitors, having to save up for a night out as the economic downturn deepened, felt they were getting less value for money from their food and drink. The traditional dish of ham supplied to 1,000 tables each seating ten people had long been notorious for being sliced so thin that it was claimed you could read the *Morning Chronicle* through it. Now, parsimony increased its transparency to such an extent that one waiter was heard to boast that he could cover the garden's entire eleven acres with slices from one ham. People complained of crude and tasteless salads, 'Lilliput' chickens and adulterated arrack punch 'warm from Vauxhall ice' which induced headaches. 'A supper at Vauxhall was a perfect abomination,' recalled Lord William Lennox, military aide to the Duke of Wellington. He added, 'Fancy walking for an hour or two round and round under a covered way, jostled by a crowd, the olfactory senses suffering from a villainous odour of oil, the ears distracted by the unmusical sounds of a noisy band or listening to comic songs of the "Pretty Polly Hopkins" stamp.'

Time for a change. And who better to restore the sparkle to this fading national treasure than the resourceful lottery man? Bish was already developing other businesses with his associates Frederick Gye and Richard Hughes, bookseller and one-time proprietor of Sadler's Wells Theatre. Typical of their ventures was the London Wine Company, which they set up to supply cut-price wines from Madeira, via complicated arrangements with agents, in competition with the fine but more expensive Cape of Good Hope wines offered by the long-established Holborn wine merchant, Thompson and Fearon. (It was considered unpatriotic for merchants to sell the even finer French wines.) Heavily promoted by placards 'in almost every thoroughfare in town' and by a newly established Association for the Suppression of Adulteration (principal members: T. Bish, F. Gye, R. Hughes), this dubious concern so provoked Thompson and Fearon that it launched a media rebuttal of the newcomer's claims. Under the apposite heading of Byron's famous dictum, 'This is the age of cant,' it published in various newspapers a long exposé of the trio's marketing methods and ridiculed their lack of wine trade expertise and experience. This worked. Within months Thompson and Fearon was able to claim their rival had 'shrunk like a weak abortion'.

The three had more success with an earlier venture, the London

Genuine Tea Company, which was launched in 1818 with the £30,000 prize that Gye had conveniently won in one of Bish's lotteries. This started to sell pre-packed, branded tea with dominant advertising and aggressive marketing that implied traditional dealers adulterated their teas. Eye-catching announcements in newspapers of often a half-column or longer, illustrated by engravings of their warehouse and supplemented by handbills and circulars, pledged to rescue the 'Tea Trade from the opprobrium attached to it by the late disclosures of adulteration'. The proprietors promised specifically 'to neither buy nor sell Bohea tea . . . so commonly used to adulterate better sorts.' Extensive advertising in local newspapers followed the bold, boastful style of the lottery adverts. One promotional item claimed 'whilst others' sent travellers to solicit orders, 'applications to sell the Company's teas are constantly arriving.' Another claimed the new firm was able to retail 'at the lowest price' due to its policy of making large purchases and taking small returns. Special offers such as free delivery within ten miles of London for cash sales also helped to win rapidly an impressive slice of the tea trade from established dealers, who resented the sly attacks on their integrity. Like Thompson and Fearon, these dealers began a public relations counter-attack, describing the newcomers as 'mere merchant-adventurers or lottery-office keepers' and emphasising their inexperience. In this case, however, the tirade only served to keep the fledgling company in the public eye and enabled it to claim that the bitter opposition of the tea dealing establishment merely proved the 'merits' of its product. Within three years the London Genuine Tea Company became the largest tea dealer in the country, employing 500 agents in every town and city. Its flagship store at 8 Charing Cross, splendidly decked out as a luxurious Chinese saloon, was one of the first High Street shops to use imaginative presentation as a way of enticing people to buy. And its use of artful national advertising to promote a prepackaged, branded and priced product (which soon superseded the grocers' traditional skills in blending and pricing tea to suit individual customers) was widely imitated.

The three were, initially, equally as successful with Vauxhall. In 1821, they bought the lease of the eight-acre site from the Tyers family, owners for nearly a century, contracting to pay a yearly ground rent averaging £1,800. There was an option to buy all the property which was exercised in 1825, when Bish dropped out as a partner. So great was the interest in the sale of the lease by auctioneer George Robins, whose showmanship always pulled in the crowds, that it was impossible to push through the crush of bidders and spectators packing out the Covent Garden saleroom. Some bidders had crossed the Channel from Paris where the event had been widely advertised. There was great excitement when the bid from the controversial London Wine Company was declared successful.

The new proprietors planned their grand relaunch for the 1822 season as most of the attractions for 1821 had already been arranged. Their ambitious Mission Statement, as it would be called today, was published prominently: 'To render Vauxhall the resort of the Noble, the Fashionable and a discerning British public.' All very well, but it needed a wheeze to draw in the crowds and it was then that Bish pulled his masterstroke. The royal name, as advertisers all know, has been brilliantly effective in helping to sell products from Josiah Wedgwood's pots 250 years ago to arms exports today. For decades the newly enthroned King George IV, first as Prince of Wales and then Prince Regent, had used Vauxhall and its conveniently dark walks as an amorous playground. Thomas Rowlandson's famous 1784 watercolour of *Vaux-Hall* shows him whispering to the actress Mary 'Perdita' Robinson, one of his many mistresses, while Georgiana, Duchess of Devonshire and other celebrities flirt and gossip.

Historians generally present him as did *The Times* when it denounced him as a rake who 'at all times would prefer a girl and a bottle to politics and a sermon' and was happy only with 'gluttony, drunkenness and gambling'. Many contemporary figures, among them Jane Austen, strongly disapproved of him. Yet he was a considerable public benefactor of the arts and patron of practically everything from the National Gallery to the Society for the Suppression of Mendacity. So society was not surprised, given his love of the gardens, that he accepted the invitation from Tom Bish, who like his father before him was a regular guest at royal parties, to become its patron. As ground landlord (he owned most of Kennington through the Duchy of Cornwall Estate) it was also in his financial interests that the venture flourished. The amusement park was promptly renamed The Royal Gardens, Vauxhall. Within days this prestigious label appeared on every entry ticket, programme, newspaper advertisement, handbill and supper menu produced by the sharp new owners. They knew that finding your message and repeating it endlessly on all possible platforms is a basic tenet of brand marketing. This is commonplace today, but a groundbreaking innovation then. Bish was one of the first, if not the first, to introduce this kind of holistic approach to advertising. They also exploited the royal connection with galas to celebrate George's birthday, his coronation, the Duke of York's Night, the Duke of Clarence's Night, ascents by the pioneering balloonist Charles Green in The Royal Vauxhall balloon, and re-enactments 'magnificent beyond description' of the Battle of Waterloo featuring more than one thousand horse and foot soldiers. Some warm summer nights virtually all of fashionable London attended, including the Duke of Wellington, Lord Palmerston, and English and overseas royalty, along with counts, lords, ladies, ambassadors and generals. And Bish made sure the newspapers reproduced all their names. With the security of royal approval (using the monarchy for marketing was not new – Josiah Wedgwood was allowed to call himself 'Potter to Her Majesty'), they enthusiastically set about rebranding, reinventing, redecorating and reviving, starting with the firework displays. These were introduced as early as 1798, but seldom met expectations.

'There were fireworks, but when they did not rise high enough, everyone laughed and said "Shocking!"' recorded a foreign visitor in 1809. Ten years later they had still not improved. 'It is certainly a very brilliant spectacle, but the fireworks are not equal to Tivoli [amusement park in Paris]' complained one spectator, society beauty Lady Calvert, in her diary. Even major events, such as the great July fete of 1813 to celebrate the battle of Vitoria when Wellington's army routed the French in Spain, saw the pyrotechnics failing to rise to the occasion, 'owing to the shortness of the time involved, the devices had not that degree of invention which belonged to such a commemoration,' observed a contemporary account.

Three firework specialists, billed as 'Signior Mortram, Chevalier Southby and Madame Hengler' were mainly responsible for these uninspiring displays, which Bish & co were determined to make more exciting. They despatched one of the three, which one is not recorded, to Paris to pick up a few tips from the experts who staged the spectacularly colourful shows that so delighted Louis XVIII, the restored Bourbon King. That envoy was almost certainly the entrepreneurial Madame Hengler, (aka Sarah Field of Lambeth), a former tightrope walker who fascinated audiences by juggling clay tobacco pipes and swallowing giant live grubs. She later became an international figure and put on her own productions in Paris, Dublin and other European cities, while supplying her celebrated fireworks for special occasions all over Britain. Her entertainment genes were passed on to her French-speaking son Henry, who, while only five years old, entertained Louis XVI and Marie Antoinette at the Paris Opera by dancing on a wire, and to later descendants who established Hengler's Victorian circuses starring her great-grandson, the famous clown Jim Frowde.

She was certainly the dominant figure; appointed 'Pyrotechnist to His Majesty' with the job of dazzling him with fireworks displays on Royal birthdays where, swathed in white garments, she presided like an ancient Greek priestess until the spectacular finale. This was a pyrotechnical presentation, in brilliant diamond characters, of the words 'G.IV, crowned July 19 1821.' No wonder she was celebrated in one of Hood's odes as 'Starry Enchantress of the Surrey Garden!'* An

* See page 199 for *Ode to Madame Hengler*.

accompanying comic woodcut represented her breasts as Catherine wheels and her ears as firecrackers. She often featured in the press. *The Observer* described the exploding squibs, pop-guns and rockets used by a mob trying to demolish an evening newspaper office in the Strand, as 'Signora Hengler herself could scarcely boast a larger magazine of pyrotechnical illustrations.' Sarah was paid huge bonuses to create new novelties to draw the crowds, such as her highly unusual Green Fire 'unknown to any other Artist', a Mine of Snakes, an Egyptian Obelisk, the Grand Girandole Wheel, Chinese Artichokes and the Temple of Fire. Favourite stunts included the tight rope walker Madame Saqui descending through a blaze of fireworks sixty feet above ground, and a 'grand imposing Scene of the Eruption of Mount Vesuvius and the Bay of Naples'. To the delight of the crowds, King George himself occasionally brandished the flaming torch that was applied to fast-burning touchpaper or cotton-wick in order to fire these entertaining set pieces. The *Gentleman's Magazine* described them as 'the most beautiful we have ever seen at these gardens.' For days before they were heralded by sandwichmen patrolling London's streets holding up large boastful placards. For once, Bish's claim that her efforts 'will exceed anything ever before exhibited in Europe' was not mere hyperbole. Britain's first systematic firework-making guide *A Manual of Pyrotechny*, published in 1824, agreed; its author, G. W. Mortimer, concluded his tome with special praise for the 'very great' merits of Vauxhall's fizz-bangs which, he said, had delighted the public and were on a larger scale than before.

The death of Madame Hengler, in 1845, was dramatic. For fifty years fireworks, manufactured elsewhere in Lambeth, had been sorted and stored in those unregulated days in her own home at 4 Asylum Buildings, Westminster Road, occasionally exploding to the annoyance and worry of local people. One dark October night a whole batch went off like an incendiary bomb. Within seconds, a sheet of flame began to sweep through the premises. Sarah, by then nearly ninety years old and enormously corpulent, was unable to raise herself to her bedroom window to jump and, crying out piteously, perished in the flames like a grotesque giant Guy Fawkes on a bonfire, a fittingly spectacular end to a remarkable career.

Bish, Gye and Hughes were responsible for many other innovations. A popular novelty was the ingenious but ludicrously named Heptaplasiesoptron, forerunner of the fairground hall of crazy mirrors, or installations by conceptual artist Anish Kapoor. This proscenium, in front of the orchestra at the Rotunda, was entirely lined with mirrors arranged so that they reflected seven times the surrounding landscaped walks, theatrical arches, revolving pillars, palm trees, fountains, artificial waterfalls, draperies, statues and supper boxes (some still decorated with paintings by William Hogarth, who was given a gold ticket for life admission). It was lit up by the latest special effects technology; the dramatic use of gas-fired lamps, which had made their world debut along Pall Mall barely fifteen years earlier. Suddenly, to the clash of cymbals and roll of drums from the orchestra, these lamps would be switched on along with 50,000 other coloured lamps, illuminated stars, chandeliers and lanterns hidden in trees throughout the gardens, creating 'a rich blaze of radiance that was a wonder to behold'.

Another innovation, and canny example of segmented marketing aimed at the family, was the introduction of 'Juvenile Fetes', featuring barnyard impressionists and Cinderella ballets, whereby all children under twelve were admitted for two shillings instead of the usual 3s 6d. On one occasion there was nearly a riot when a crowd of 'vulgar-looking' old women from Wapping gatecrashed a performance, blocked the view of hundreds of children and refused to move despite repeated requests to do so.

'Coloured' singers such as Madame Georgiana were another novelty as Bish ruthlessly dumped tired acts like the singer Charles Dignum. 'Much interest was excited by the first appearance of a Lady of Colour, a native of Calcutta. She accompanies herself on the piano forte with great taste and spirit,' said one approving press report. An interesting new drink was added to the ample supplies of burgundy, champagne,

Fireworks specialist Madame Hengler (aka Sarah Field of Lambeth) – one of several female entrepreneurs hired by Bish to liven up Vauxhall. She is seen her, with jumping crackers for her ears and Catherine wheels for her breasts, in a woodcut illustrating Thomas Hood's 1830 ode to her

The Prince of Wales and Duchess of Devonshire are among fashionable revellers seen here carousing at Vauxhall in its heyday. By 1820 the pleasure ground had declined, but Bish and Gye revived and rebranded it (Rowlandson, 1785)

claret, hock, Madeira, Rhenish, sherry, arrack punch, port, cider and beer carted in from the cellars of the London Wine Company. This is simply listed as 'stout', and was probably Guinness, which was then making its first forays into the London market.

An advertising blitz preceded the brash new owners' relaunch. With their typical aggressive marketing methods they promised everything would be bigger, better and more amazing than before, resulting in 'a combination of talent and wonders that were never seen till now'. They had just months to make good this promise before the park was reopened, under royal patronage, on 3 June 1822. The crowds, curious to experience the new Vauxhall, poured in. The season was a triumph. The press raved over the transformation, congratulating 'the loyal and enterprising proprietors' and claiming 'too much praise cannot be given to them'. Another review declared, 'The varieties are now so numerous and follow with such rapid succession that they cannot fail to awaken and occupy the attention of the most careless lounger.' No other ground could equal it, not even Bath's acclaimed Sydney Gardens. When Hood paid a visit to Finch's park in Norwich, he wrote that he found it 'a sort of twopenny Vauxhall where I laughed heartily at the ridiculous attempt to rival Bish & co'. The relaunch was not universally popular. A Kingston magistrate called Briscoe objected to the renewal of the license on the grounds that he had observed 'disgusting scenes ... scenes that no modest female could witness'. As this seems to have been merely boisterous mixed sex dancing, the other magistrates overruled him and granted the license.

For their part the trio pledged that for the future, 'No personal trouble nor pecuniary considerations will deter us from selecting and introducing every novelty.' They were as good as their word. Profits soared, allowing bigger and better attractions to be bought as they continued to invest heavily in promotion until their weekly expenses of £800 regularly included £100 for printing and advertisements. There was a record-breaking attendance of nearly 135,000 for the following 1823 season, with receipts amounting to £29,590.

Overseeing the attractions was a comical Dickensian master of ceremonies called C. H. Simpson, who greeted visitors with exaggerated obsequiousness wearing an eighteenth-century frock coat with black silk knee breeches and carrying a tasseled and silver-headed cane. 'He was continually bowing to everyone he met,' recalled the journalist John Richardson, 'and the incessant moving of his arm and the hat at the end of it resembled the motion of a parish pump-handle in full play'. Although he cut a rather absurd figure with his constant bowing and scraping, Simpson was a popular fixture of Vauxhall for thirty-five years; the novelist Thackeray called him, with affection, 'that kind, smiling, idiot', Robert Cruikshank, brother of George, commemorated him in a print, and from 1833 a huge forty-five-foot-high effigy of him in coloured lamps was exhibited by the Rotunda. Later, he was the inspiration for the 'Striding Man' logo on Johnnie Walker whisky labels. Bish, who made a point of patrolling the illuminated avenues on busy nights, was particularly protective when rowdy customers picked on this eccentric, a natural victim with his short stature and face pitted with smallpox beneath effeminate well-powdered hair. Late one Monday evening in July during the 1822 season, three London drapers, the brothers William and John Creed, and Edmund Lancaster entered the gardens dressed up in the exact costumes of Tom, Jerry and Logic, stars of the stage version of *Real Life in London*, then running to packed audiences at the Adelphi Theatre off the Strand. Drunk on punch and wine, they roared around the walks all night, knocking off hats, yelling in ears and shoulder charging 'many persons of distinction'. Simpson was sent to stop this antisocial behaviour and have the trio arrested by the police on duty but, according to *The Times,* his intervention 'produced no other effect than that of exasperating them to a more offensive line of conduct,' and they continued to act out the disreputable conduct of their theatrical heroes until a Mr. Hall and his officers overpowered them and dragged them out to the watchhouse.

At the subsequent court hearing, Bish declared 'the proprietors are resolved to have the gardens most vigilantly watched, and to punish every person who disturbs the company'. The magistrate, Mr. Chambers, congratulated him on his determination to bring such offenders to justice, although on this occasion it was decided to drop the prosecution if the belligerent actors manqué paid forty shillings each to The Distressed Irish fund, Bish's favourite charity. That same month a drunk aristocrat clad in Highland dress ran amok, brandishing a dirk and a loaded pistol, 'behaving towards ladies in the most crude and indecorous manner'. In the confusion, during which he tried to shoot one of the watchmen trying to apprehend him, he managed to escape from the grounds.

This determination to enforce good order illustrates Bish's hands-on approach to all his ventures. Yet in his love of precision and detail, he never forgot the broad strategic sweep, a rare combination that was to make his fortune. An anonymous note of the period specifically credits him not only with building the important Colonnade entrance in Kennington Lane but, much more significantly, with upgrading 'Orchestra, Ballet, Theatre etc.' Culturally, that went way beyond the new, well-received, vaudeville acts such as the Indian sword swallower Ramoo Sammee, aerial acrobat Juan Bellinck 'the infant flying devil', Signor Nestarsi de Verani's one-man band and the French mechanical theatre 'with hydraulics much improved by Mr. Morris'. Plays specially designed for the gardens were commissioned from the playwright James Robinson Planché (later Vauxhall's musical director), and operas from the composer Henry Rowley Bishop of 'Home, Sweet Home' fame. World-class conductors like Monsieur Hullis of the Royal Academy of Music at Paris were contracted to conduct the concerts. A moving spirit was Vauxhall's scandalous singing star Madame Vestris, who first sang there in 1826, famed both for her sweet renderings of 'Cherry Ripe', one of the greatest hits of all time, and for her legendary long shapely legs that had captivated a series of rich lovers, including Bish's political ally the radical MP Thomas Duncombe. The Italian temptress, more prosaically known by her married name of Mrs. Matthews, was not loved by everyone. 'She has noodled several foolish fellows to spend large sums of money on her,' sniffed social reformer Francis Place in his diary. He complained one of her Drury Lane performances was 'a vulgar low lived piece' got up only to show off her legs. Lucia Elizabeth Vestris, granddaughter of the engraver Francesco Bartolozzi, was not just a pretty face. Like Madame Hengler, she was a shrewd businesswoman who graduated from performer to tycoon, using good looks, a sharp brain and phenomenal energy to advance her career. She became the first actress-manager on the London stage, modernising and professionalising it to European standards in order to meet the expectations of increasingly discerning middle-class audiences. Covent Garden was among a number of theatres she transformed and made fashionable through consistently high acting standards, proper rehearsals, beautifully designed scenery, theatrical innovation such as the introduction of Weber's operas, along with comfortable seats. For women particularly, theatre-going became a pleasant experience and less like visiting a bear garden. At Vauxhall and before she became nationally famous, her intellect and looks helping advance a cultural revolution which, as London's growing population increasingly demanded new and varied entertainment, eventually transmuted into theatres, circuses and music halls.

As 1825 drew to a close, all looked set fair for the thriving Tom Bish, who was employing, directly or indirectly, more than 1,400 people. He had made a success of Vauxhall Gardens (resigning his partnership with Gye and Hughes in July after making a good profit), had amassed a fortune, and could afford to live in a St. James Square mansion grander than the Piccadilly town house acquired by the financier Rothschild. He was feted in the media, portrayed in prints such as the caricaturist Richard Dighton's 'A View from Cornhill', respected in the Stock Exchange, took the waters with members of the aristocracy at the spa town of Buxton in the Peak District, promenaded with them along the seafront at a Brighton made highly fashionable by King George IV, and was tipped for a seat in Parliament. In that time-honoured phrase, what could possibly go wrong? The answer lay in events 6,000 miles away. Miners and metalworkers in Mexico, Peru, Brazil and Columbia were not delivering the riches widely expected by wildly optimistic investors in the City of London, who had made huge loans to the newly liberated Latin American republics. This helped to trigger a catastrophic financial crisis – the worst of the nineteenth century – which bankrupted many entrepreneurs. Among them was Tom Bish.

"Okay, so we'll broadcast the advert for loo paper just after the banks announce their annual results"

CHAPTER NINE

Annus Horribilis

Bish's career as a stockbroker was chequered. Once, an insolvent corn chandler called John Penrice accused him of absconding with his wife's money while she was still a client. And he was forever being hauled before the elders of the Stock Exchange to explain his various misdemeanours. In 1819, the General Purposes Committee ordered him to pay James Vandsommer £2.50 interest on an India Bond that he had earlier declined to honour. A year earlier he had blatantly broken regulations by setting up the London Genuine Tea Company, with his old cronies Gye and Hughes. This was incompatible with his role as a dealer in tea stocks; he was forced to withdraw formally from the business, despite some cunning delaying tactics on his part, and it is clear that he continued to advise on advertising tactics. Worse was to come when, on 26 August 1819, he defaulted on his Exchange debts, though on this occasion his fifty-nine creditors issued a statement saying they had received ten shillings in the pound on their respective debts and satisfactory security for payment of the remainder. The committee appointed to examine the accounts reported, however, 'That in consequence of his (Bish) having destroyed several documents relating to his Account, we are not able to ascertain his situation very accurately.' Despite this decidedly dubious action he was, eventually, readmitted to the Exchange after several unsuccessful attempts to rejoin. Unfortunately for him his re-entry, on 21 November 1825, could not have been more badly timed.

The great City panic in the winter of 1825 and its aftershocks for the next eighteen months ranks with the 1926 Wall Street crash and the 2008 credit crunch crisis as one of the worst financial disasters ever to destabilise the British economy. In a re-run of the South Sea Bubble of 1720, some shares in worthless get rich quick schemes in Latin America shot up by 1700 percent in a few months. Joint stock company mania mirrored foreign loan mania. 'People are speculating mad. Shares are to be had in anything you may fancy from Gas to Oysters,' wrote one contemporary commentator as speculators shelled out more than £18 million, ranging from £2,872,000 for the Mexican loan to £1,000 for the Lower Rhine Steam company. The bubble burst in December. All over England inadequately capitalised country banks collapsed dramatically after printing too many banknotes (an early example of 'quantitative easing') which they could not honour. The entire banking system came near to collapse, leading to widespread personal insolvencies and serious riots as the police fought panicking crowds jamming the streets of the city of London, where the main banking houses were located. At the height of the crisis the Bank of England had just 8,000 gold sovereigns left in its vaults before the cavalry arrived in the form of massive shipments of gold sovereigns from Paris. 'The state of the City and the terror of all the bankers and merchants as well as of all owners of property is not to be conceived but by those who witnessed it,' wrote an official at the heart of government, Charles Greville, Clerk to the Privy Council. So catastrophic was the failure of both foreign government bonds and joint stock company shares that only Brazil was still paying interest by December 1828, while in Europe Greece, Portugal and Spain had all defaulted; only a fifth (127) of joint stock companies survived to the end of 1826. Greed and folly, compounded by ineffective State actions which swung between doing nothing to banning virtually any kind of credit, had ensured a disaster that destroyed many lives. Initially, his lottery profits sheltered Bish from the worst of the financial storm.

Although Parliament had banned lotteries, it allowed one final draw which eventually took place on 18 October 1826, at Cooper's Hall in the City of London. Four teams of lottery contractors got together to plan it and put up £720,000 in additional prize money, proposing nine single day draws spread over fourteen months. Bish, individualistic as ever, went it alone with a separate, and very profitable, scheme.

A massive advertising campaign preceded the draw, which was initially due to take place on Tuesday 18 July 1826. Handbills, erroneously describing the event as 'positively the last lottery that will ever be drawn in England,' were distributed in streets all over London and placed under door knockers. Many colour or black and white circulars featuring lottery alphabets and humorous verses were also thrust under the noses of passers-by. Newspapers ran ingenious advertisements from rival brokers whose offices were decorated with lanterns. There were noisy parades of men with sandwich boards, poles, and purple silk banners embossed in large gold letters, usually accompanied by bellmen, bands of trumpets, clarinets, and horns. Brightly decorated carts proclaimed the launch of schemes which vied with each other in extravagant claims. Stars of the processions were a painted carriage representing a giant Lottery Wheel drawn by two prancing dappled grey horses, and a square carriage surmounted by a gilt imperial crown. The adverts announced that after an uninterrupted period of 132 years: 'ALL LOTTERIES END FOR EVER ON TUESDAY NEXT!'

The draw was postponed, however, until 18 October because the contractors claimed they needed more time to get rid of unsold tickets. This seems strange as there had been demands the previous year for a parliamentary enquiry into the inflated number of tickets sold; 200,000 as opposed to the original 40,000, according to 'VINDEX' in a letter to *The Times*. The anonymous author, presumably suspecting a dummy numbers ruse, alleged the contractors had already 'managed to appropriate to themselves an immense profit'. Whatever the truth, they used questionable methods such as arbitrarily raising the price of tickets to promote the idea they were in great demand when sales were actually flagging.

The draw, carried out as usual by the Bluecoat boys from Christ's Hospital, was an anticlimax. No major prizes were won and the fact that more than half the tickets remained unsold proved the Treasury's case that the game had lost the support of the public. The real winners were the contractors. Although Bish made a considerable sum from this last gasp of the lottery, it was not enough to stem his stock market losses, which began to turn into a flood. He found it increasingly difficult to pay his debts, although he continued to be a generous giver to charitable causes, such as the Lord Mayor of London's appeal for relief of the manufacturing towns. Early in March 1827, the porter stationed at the Stock Exchange door gave three loud knocks with a mallet and announced: 'Mr. Bish presents his respects to the house and regrets to state he is unable to comply with his bargains.'[contracts]. For the second time he had defaulted, and on a much larger scale than before. His debt was £15,789 7s 6d (£800,000 today), much more than was normal for a defaulter.

Another stockbroker by the name of George Carroll, a former lottery contractor who had been in fierce competition with Bish, exchanging rancorous insults with him in the media on occasion, most generously tried to bail him out, paying six shillings and eight pence in the pound to creditors. The position remained, however, very unclear, with some creditors complaining that they had not been paid. The General Purposes Committee summoned Bish to a meeting on 5 March, but was told he had left London for the bedside of his sick daughter Frances Elizabeth. He also declined to attend a second meeting on 16 March, pleading two deaths in his family. At this point the elders lost patience and voted to expel him, announcing this in the traditional way by painting his name in large letters on a blackboard hung high above the trading floor for all to see.

So severely did looming financial disaster shake Bish's self-control that he allowed himself to become embroiled in an extraordinary road rage incident on London Bridge, resulting in his prosecution. On Wednesday 16 August 1826 he appeared before the Lord Mayor, William Venables, at Mansion House charged with assaulting C. J. Willett, a shoemaker who worked in the seedy, overcrowded Borough district south of the river Thames. The dilapidated, 650-year-old bridge, was a nightmare to cross. It was showing great signs of wear and tear, had never fully recovered from the extensive damage wrought by the legendary severe frost of 1814 and was so narrow and congested that it was on this thoroughfare that the 'keep left' rule of the road was first adopted. Another hazard was the gangs of male teenaged pickpockets who crept behind the slow-moving gigs to lift silk handkerchiefs trailing from the pockets of the coat-tails of unsuspecting riders. Hundreds of the stolen items were to be seen hanging on long poles projecting from the windows of virtually every house in nearby Field Lane. Five or six shillings was the usual recovery fee.

Whether Bish wished to avoid this notorious toll or was merely impatient to get over is not disclosed in the court records. What is clear is that as Willett was dragging his heavy cart, Bish suddenly lashed him twice with his whip. The indignant shoemaker attempted to get the name of his assailant who ignored his shouts and drove on, only to get caught up in a traffic jam of horse-drawn vehicles. When Willett grabbed hold of the rails of the gig, Bish lashed him again, very hard this time, and beat him on the knuckles with the butt end of his whip. 'I then used bad language,' Willett told the Lord Mayor, 'which I ought not to have made use of towards such a gentleman, but I was greatly irritated and could not help it.'

Throughout the proceedings Bish put on the rather patronising smile which was later to so irritate his fellow MPs and provoke some newspapers to describe him as 'looking dead nuts on himself' (the crude modern equivalent is 'up his own arse'). He knew Venables, a papermaker and stationer like Bish Senior, both socially and professionally, and may have been counting on City solidarity to get him off. 'Why my lord,' he drawled 'the fact is that I was going over the bridge with a spirited horse; there were two lines of carts and carriages, with room enough for me to pass but this man here, who was following behind a wagon got out of the ranks before me and prevented me from passing. I called out to him repeatedly but he paid no attention to me and I certainly did give him a cut or two, as he states, for my horse was very spirited, and might have been restive. He afterwards came up and would have created a deal of disturbance.' Willett, described as 'very peaceably disposed and modest,' denied that he ever drew out of his rank. Venables, an independent-minded and highly respected businessman, who was applauded for the way he had steadied City nerves during the great financial crash, chose to believe him rather than Bish. 'Even those who drag trucks are human beings,' he said, 'and they are not disposed to bear quietly the application of the whip, especially when they are not conscious of having merited it.'

This humiliating put-down of a colleague who barely eight months ago had been elected, for the first time, as a common councilman for Cornhill ward in the city of London made no dent on the huge ego before him. 'Well my lord, if you think so,' he replied. 'I have no objection to pay this man any money that will satisfy him. I would rather do that to get rid of the thing and not be troubled any more about it.' Venables agreed and the case was settled for an undisclosed sum of damages.

When Bish was thrown out of the Stock Exchange, *Bell's Life in London & Sporting Chronicle* observed, 'Mr. Bish may now, with cause, exclaim, "A plague on both your Houses," for his house speculations seem to have been altogether unfortunate. It is to be hoped he has reserved a nest egg on which to lay the foundation of better fortune thereafter.' The other 'house' referred to was Parliament. With the demise of lotteries getting nearer, it became increasingly urgent to find other income to fund his extravagant lifestyle, hence his buccaneering business forays with Frederick Gye into tea, wine, pleasure gardens

and, on his own account, the theatre. This last proved a disaster. In
June 1826, as a so-called 'spirited investor', Bish was highest bidder at
an auction of the debt-ridden Drury Lane Theatre, and signed a lease to
pay an annual rent of £12,500 for fourteen years. He hired Alfred Bunn,
responsible for previous brilliant seasons, as manager despite persistent
rumours that he was in a homosexual relationship, then a capital crime,
with an unnamed colonel. Actors were hired, including the tragedian
William Charles Macready, scenery painted and the Needlemakers
livery company held a jolly celebration dinner at which Bish made
'a very neat and apposite speech'. Only two weeks after striking the
deal, however, probably realising he had overcommitted himself, he
suddenly sacked Bunn amid 'much hurly-burly,' announcing that he no
longer intended to be lessee. The furious Drury Lane trustees refused
to release him and there were acrimonious rows until an American
impresario called Stephen Price 'of coarse manners, repulsive conduct
and vulgar conversation' agreed to take on the lease and honour the
performers' contracts in exchange for receiving Bish's forfeited £2,000
deposit. This released a torrent of xenophobia in the London press
which, fifty years after independence, still regarded the 'Yankees' as
uncouth colonials; 'most degrading ... a general slur against the nation'
was one of the more polite comments. Ironically Price, having rescued
Bish from financial ruin, was himself bankrupted by the huge costs of
running the jinxed theatre which over the years became a concert hall,
a French hippodrome, a pantomime centre and even a circus venue, in
doomed attempts to pay its way.

Bish calculated that becoming a Member of Parliament would not
only increase his social status but provide a useful base for making
money. That was why late in 1825 he made characteristically careful
preparations for a political career as a reformer, setting his sights on
the constituency of Leominster in Herefordshire, a remote market
town with the dubious distinction of being the last place in England to
use a ducking stool (a surprisingly large contraption which had its final
outing in 1809 and is still kept on display in the local Priory Church).

Leominster was twenty hours by coach from London and a favourite choice of rich City men as votes could be bought for five to ten guineas each. 'Thomas Bish of London arrived in this city [Worcester] this evening on route to Leominster, for which borough he starts at the next election in the Whig interest,' announced the *Worcester Journal* on one December. Six weeks later, the newspaper reported he was 'distributing among the poor, indiscriminately, tea, sugar, meat and drapery,' along with 1,000 blankets. He followed this up with free beef and bread served twice a week to 1,300 voters (out of a population of 4,000), and threw open the Royal Oak public house in South Street not only for as much beer and cider that the voters could drink but for lavish 'canvassing suppers'. This largesse went down well at a time of severe recession in Herefordshire, with poor crops and low prices. Wool, a stable trade of Leominster, had halved in price over the year while a mainstay industry, glove-making, was beginning to decline from its heyday when 900 people were employed stitching the elegant gloves in their homes. 'We have never seen such days as them since, sir,' said an old recipient of the bribes in a newspaper article twenty years later. A witness in a complicated 1832 case at Hereford Assizes over an unpaid-for election chair (the very one used to parade Bish on his victory tour) put it rather differently: 'Leominster was always venal and corrupt.' Indirect bribery also came in the form of paying the rates of voters in order to register them as being qualified to vote at elections. (Qualifications for voting in the boroughs varied widely; some were much more 'rotten' than others.) Bish's involvement in this particular form of corruption was revealed by a solicitor John James, former Liberal election agent for Hereford county, in evidence to the 1835 parliamentary enquiry into election bribery. Its comprehensive 1,000-page report details how all candidates regularly gave suppers, food and drink to Leominster voters for up to fourteen months before the poll and how Bish, in particular, instructed his election agent to pay their rates, unlike nearby Hereford where such practices were frowned upon. Such measures were probably necessary given the ruthlessness of his Tory opponents. Their favourite tactic was to hire scores of thugs to force men from their homes, make them drunk and hold them prisoner until 'bewildered and, in many cases, unconscious' they signed a pledge to support the anti-reform candidate. So extensive was this kind of malpractice that Sir John Campbell, a prominent reformer who later became Attorney-General, declared in 1832, 'it is a disgrace to be born in Leominster'.

The resourceful entrepreneur also gave practical help. When the town's Coleman Bank collapsed in March 1826, with hundreds of other country banks during the great financial panic, it deprived the town of ready cash. 'The whole country is in distress from the absence of circulating medium for the common purposes of life,' wrote Greville. No banknotes were accepted, only gold. On hearing of the crisis and anticipating his wishes, Bish's brother-in-law Mr. Wean, who had married his sister Elizabeth, swiftly travelled from London with several thousand gold sovereigns. These he gave as a temporary loan to any Leominster person who applied, in exchange for Coleman banknotes, to be repaid without interest and at the borrower's convenience. A day later Bish himself, though in ill health, hurried up with more sovereigns from Brighton, where he was recuperating, and exchanged several hundred for banknotes handed over by grateful market day crowds. 'This at once supplied the town with circulating medium; and the relief afforded was in many cases very essential as the distress was beyond conception,' said the *Bristol Mercury*.

When Parliament was dissolved in June for the 1826 general election, the Bish publicity machine swung rapidly into action. An advert addressed to 'The Electors of Leominster' appeared in *The Morning Chronicle* promising: 'No interested motive, no mean individual advantage shall ever induce me to compromise your independence.' Highly ornamental cards were distributed. They read 'Mr. Bish, Candidate to represent in Parliament the Ancient and Independent Borough of LEOMINSTER, solicits the Honour of your Vote and Interest.' The *Glasgow Herald* claimed: 'Lucky Bish, the gentleman who sold the first £30,000 and the last £30,000 they say, is certain of his return. ... Should Mr. Bish take an active part in Parliament, there can be no doubt of his speedy promotion to the financial department of administration – he has been so many years the ex-Parliamentary CHANCE-SELLER OF THE EXCHEQUER.'

Like an emperor entering ancient Rome, his arrival at the hustings was triumphal. Two miles from Leominster his 'travelling chariot' was greeted by a huge crowd, including many ladies excited by the prospect of having such a celebrity in their midst. The enthusiastic females took the horses from Bish's carriage, he clambered on the box and he was then pulled through the streets of the town where every window was crowded with other well-dressed ladies wearing his colours of green, orange and blue. Some displayed blankets pinned with cockades, others waved flags with inscriptions such as 'BISH, the Friend of the People' and 'Bish and Independence'. On arrival at the Royal Oak, the Whigs' campaign headquarters, he made a short speech gallantly attributing his certain success 'chiefly to the kind interest you ladies have shown in my favour'. They could not vote, of course, but would have influenced their husbands' choice. 'We have often felt the attractive power of the ladies of England' declared the magazine *John Bull*, 'but never till Lucky Bish went to Leominster was it ever actually ascertained how the ladies drew the men after them.'

Bish spent at least £12,000 (£500,000 today) on his campaign, twice the average going rate of £6,000 but much less than the £50,000 necessary to buy some other constituencies in those pre-reform days. This expenditure and his personal charm won him one of the borough's two seats when the result was finally declared on 15 June. A popular Waterloo war hero, Lord Hotham, won the other seat for the Tories, topping the poll with 557 votes followed by Bish (445), the London banker Rowland Stephenson (254) and an unknown City gent of Grosvenor Square called Frederick Cuthbert (57). The ladies hoisted their conquering hero on a huge chair decked with ribbons and paraded him around the town with banners and ribbons through large crowds of cheering well-wishers. Five days later he joined other newly elected liberal Whigs, including Gye, who had won Chippenham, for noisy celebrations over dinner at the Albion Tavern in London, hosted by Matthew Wood, radical MP for the City of London and one-time friend of Queen Caroline. His victory was short-lived. Like many very talented people, Bish could be 'too clever by half'', in politician Iain Macleod's famous phrase. He must have known that he could not, under the law, be a Member of Parliament at the same time as benefiting financially from holding a contract with the government on the provision of public services. Perhaps he thought that the lottery fell in the category of 'public amusements', a view that won him some media support. Perhaps he thought that assigning his lottery business to his son-in-law, the blameless Rev. Robert Hodgson Fowler, on the morning of the election 'in consideration of natural love and affectation and ten shillings' would avoid a tricky conflict of interest. He miscalculated badly in thinking he could have it both ways. On polling day, his main opponent Stephenson questioned his eligibility to stand on the grounds he was a lottery contractor. During two previous parliamentary contests, where he had stood as a candidate, the banker had challenged the result, unsuccessfully. This time he won. After long and complex arguments from both sides, during which Stephenson's lawyer Coleridge argued the assignment was fraudulent, the returning officer supported the challenge and declared 'a double entry' (leaving it to MPs to decide who was to join them as the member). It was the first occasion for a century that this had happened in a parliamentary election. Gloom and disappointment spread over the faces of Bish and his supporters as the candidates prepared to address the electors. 'Mr. Bish spoke at great length and with great bitterness,' reported *The Times*, 'from notes written on the backs of old lottery cards on which Bish & Co, with flourishes of blue and red, were very visible'.

The double entry was referred to a commons committee who decided, in February 1827, that a contract did exist. So Bish, who had not endeared himself to his fellow MPs by accusing them of

hypocrisy in banning the lucky draw while they continued to gamble in
St. James's clubs, was unseated and Stephenson declared the member.
Hood rubbed this in with a satirical ode:

> Election chances seem'd a vent
> For thy desires – Parliament
> Is not so easily won: -
> Numbers were once to thee a treat
> But now by numbers thou wert beat
> And by Rowland Stephenson

Bish had the last laugh. The self-righteous Stephenson, once lauded
as 'safer than the Bank of England', turned out to be a conman. The
following year he fled under the assumed name of Smith to Savannah in
Georgia, with £58,000 in cash from his Lombard Street banking house,
causing it to crash at a time when there were no government bail-outs.
As news of his flight scandalised the nation, the *Derby Mercury* reported,
'Mr. Bish of lottery fame has again offered to represent Leominster,
in the room [place] of Stephenson, the runaway banker.' Eventually,
the fugitive was tracked down, arrested and kept in a debtor's prison in
New York until he was formally bankrupted on 19 January 1830, and
thus automatically expelled from the House of Commons. Within days
of the expulsion, Bish threw his hat in the ring and resumed courting
the constituency. Although he received a warm welcome from the
assorted cider-makers, glovers, hatters, tanners, soap boilers, farmers
and traders, he did not as expected stand at that year's general election,
which the Tories lost to the Whigs. Instead, the electors returned an
unworldly working-class tallow chandler, Thomas Brayen, who hated
the club-like atmosphere at Westminster and resigned within months.
'We trust we are not to lose Tommy-chandler from the House, and
particularly if we are to have an am-bish-ous ex-lottery office-keeper,'
commented *The Age*. Again, Bish unaccountably withdrew at the start
of polling at the next general election in 1831, which resulted in a
Whig landslide and further strong popular support for parliamentary
reform.

Ever since sabre-wielding cavalrymen killed twenty protestors and injured hundreds more at a huge pro-reform demonstration on St. Peter's Field in Manchester in 1819, immediately dubbed the Peterloo Massacre, the campaign for political, economic and social changes grew and intensified. Inequality bred serious disorder. In autumn 1830, the Tory home secretary Sir Robert Peel had to advise King William IV to cancel his visit to the City of London for a Lord Mayor's day celebration because of intelligence that radicals planned to storm the Tower of London, seize weapons and kill him. The following year drunken mobs rampaged through London, Derby, Nottingham and Bristol, which they occupied for three days, setting fire to the City's Mansion House and Bishop's Palace. The country came close to revolution before, after fierce opposition from the Tory-dominated House of Lords led by Wellington (angry Londoners later pelted him with mud and excreta in the streets), the Whigs' great Reform Act finally became law on 8 June 1832. Although debate continues as to how radical this historic legislation ically was (only one in seven men had the vote and all women remained disqualified from voting), at the time anti-reform aristocrats regarded the measure as a prelude to trundling out the tumbrils. It swept away all the notorious rotten boroughs like Old Sarum, a ruined mound in Wiltshire, laid the foundations for a uniform franchise, gave parliamentary seats to previously unrepresented, rapidly expanding, industrial towns such as Birmingham and Manchester, and gave the vote to men owning or occupying property valued at ten pounds a year or more. Reform was slow to reach Leominster, despite the efforts of the town council, who spent £150 making a new survey map and valuation of all rateable property. Fewer that 200 ten-pound households were added to the electorate and, in the ensuing general election of December 1832, two candidates were returned without a contest, 'both paying the usual head of money to the voters,' according to one report. One was Lord Hotham. The other was Tom Bish.

"The only difference between actors
and politicians is that actors sometimes
believe what they're saying"

CHAPTER TEN

The Fight Back

Commentators often overuse the term 'political earthquake', but there is no better way of describing the result of the general election of 1832. It rocked Britain to its constitutional foundations. A parliament was returned of 510 reformers (Whigs 320, Radicals and Irish 190) compared with a mere 150 Tories, giving the Grey government a massive majority of 360 for imposing comprehensive change. Into that newly reformed assembly came corn merchants, butchers, entrepreneurs, squires, lawyers, the radical journalist William Cobbett, even a prizefighter-turned-successful racehorse owner called John Gully, and self-made manufacturers like Josiah Wedgwood, son of the potter Josiah. The triumph of the mercantile and professional middle classes over the old landed aristocracy incited the Tory press to fury. In a sneering and exaggerated tirade, *The Age* complained that 'the intrusion of mercers, haberdashers, soap-boilers, cheesemongers, rag-merchants and coalheavers' into the Commons had made the place so common 'as to be little better than a Trades' Political Union on a grand scale'.

The new men are commemorated in Sir George Hayter's famous painting, now in London's National Portrait Gallery, which depicts their first session on 5 February 1833 in St. Stephen's Chapel, the original Commons Chamber later destroyed by fire. There they sit grouped on the left (Tories on the right), in their uniform of frock coats, stiff white collars, waistcoats and fashionable pumps, mainly unsmiling but looking confident and rather pleased with themselves. Bish, hair greying now, has a rather anxious air. This was uncharacteristic, as he habitually wore a rather superior expression that annoyed his fellow legislators and lost him their support for his political campaigns. *The Satirist*, the *Private Eye* of the day, described him sarcastically as 'the most able, the most brilliant, the most intellectual, the most powerful man in the British legislature'. He also could never shake off his reputation as a chancer among some of his contemporaries such as Thomas Allsop, one of Coleridge's circle, who described him as 'a very dirty person'.

Another image of him from this period shows him sporting a monocle on a long black cord suspended from his neck. Seated in a red upholstered chair and wearing black coat and waistcoat he looks suitably statesmanlike in this miniature he thought appropriate to commission, as if to assert his status. This little portrait was gilt-mounted within a brown leather travelling case and became a treasured heirloom of his daughter Fanny's family until the line died out in the early twenty-first century. George Robins, who had presided so theatrically over the famous 1821 auction of Vauxhall Pleasure Gardens, successfully proposed him for membership of the newly established Garrick Club. This was named after the eighteenth-century actor David Garrick, who was as skilful a self-promoter as Bish, presenting his image to the world through 500 different engravings and pictures over his lifetime. In homage to the great thespian, the club's pre-dinner apartment was called 'the green room', a green curtain divided the dining room, the courses were called 'acts' and dinner comings and goings were termed 'entrances' and 'exits'. By 1834, the year Bish was elected to it, this convivial Covent Garden watering hole had become the fashionable haunt not only of actors but writers, musicians, barristers and politicians, particularly reformers such as Lord John Russell and radicals like Thomas Duncombe. Then, as now, there were complaints about lawyers taking over the club; Alfred Bunn, Bish's occasional

A miniature of Tom Bish, circa 1830 (with thanks to the Luke Bodalbhai
Collection UK, courtesy of Bonhams)

partner in theatrical ventures, claimed it had degenerated into a 'Junior Law Club'.

Despite the jibes, Bish became a hard-working legislator, popular with his constituents. Tremendous and prolonged cheering greeted mention of his name during a splendid dinner at Leominster's Red Lion inn to celebrate the passing of the Reform Act. 'Tom Bish,' said the local worthy proposing his health, 'has always been a friend not only to the poor but to the borough at large, and at a time when his assistance was truly desirable'. Many of those applauding were among 500 electors who had clubbed together to buy him an elegant silver tureen 'in testimony of their great respect and esteem" after he was expelled from the seat in 1826. The dull, unlit, streets of rural Leominster, where gas-lamps were not installed until 1835 and where only two stagecoaches a day called, was a world away from the bustling clubs of the West End and the dining taverns of the City of London. Yet he regularly made the tedious two-day journey there from London, and took up his voters' causes, such as presenting to Parliament their petition for the abolition of slavery in Britain's colonies. As he pledged in a letter to them, 'I am an Enemy to Slavery in all Countries and States, no matter what may be the complexion of its victims – black or white.' He organised the Leominster hunt ball, showered money on local charities and good causes from the town's Mechanics' Benefit Club to the Herefordshire Female Servants' Reward Society and communicated very effectively with his constituents through regular 'addresses' published in the newspaper columns of local newspapers. The new MP proved his commitment by building a house on the outskirts of the town in such an out of the way spot that it was still known as 'Bish's folly' at the start of the twentieth century. While the *Morning Chronicle* was quick to damn him as 'one of the promoters of anarchy and national bankruptcy', he always denied being an 'out and outer' [colloquial term for a radical] although on one occasion he was one of the very few members who voted to allow recreations on Sunday, then considered a shocking proposal. As a mainstream reformer, Bish conscientiously supported the government in the division lobbies (twice missing key votes by accidentally getting locked in the library, however), voting to ban capital punishment, military flogging, the press ganging of seamen, and also to clean up corruption in the armed forces and other State agencies. He campaigned vigorously for the abolition of grossly inflated and unmerited pensions pocketed by state officials which successive Tory governments had encouraged. With Gladstone's brother Thomas, a fellow MP, he sat on various committees of enquiry into election bribery at places like Liverpool and Warwick, presumably managing to keep a straight face. He was proud of his voting record, and showed his Pooterish tendency by writing obsessively to *The Times* whenever that newspaper made a mistake; on 27 June 1833, he complained to the editor that 'I did not, as reported, vote on the 147th clause of the Church Temporalities Bill [major measure to reform the Church of Ireland] because of an accident that detained me in Hertfordshire.' On another occasion he complained to the Editor of the *Cheltenham Free Press* for incorrectly stating he had missed crucial parliamentary votes, and pointed out, 'your paper has an extensive circulation in Cheltenham where I have many friends'. He was equally quick to quash rumours in his constituency, once distributing circulars to the voters stating 'there is not a word of truth in the report of my intended retirement'. Campaigns for a secret ballot in parliamentary elections, shortening the duration of parliaments and publishing 'authenticated reports' of its proceedings won his support as did much wider reforms in Church, judiciary, penal code, factory conditions, poor laws and child welfare. All this he did at a time when his wife Mary had fallen ill, though he assiduously nursed her in the last few weeks of her life in Brighton where she died in January 1834. (Shortly after her death he himself fell seriously ill and did not return to the House of Commons until early March.) Bish also backed early attempts to repeal the Corn Laws, the hated duties which protected English landowners against cheaper imported corn and forced workers in fast-growing towns to pay higher bread prices.

Their eventual abolition was a triumph for the newly elected middle-class politicians. As an expert witness in many fraud trials featuring forged financial instruments, banknotes and lottery tickets, he used his specialist knowledge in a campaign to make the Bank of England design notes so that it was much harder to forge them. Outside Westminster he was equally energetic, campaigning for the repeal of the window tax by organising letters sent to potential sympathisers nationwide, and enthusiastically helping to professionalise the fledgling Liberal Party born out of the Reform coalition of Whigs and Radicals. Professional electioneering, with committed candidates, local party workers, election agents, constituency associations and sophisticated political propaganda, including manifestos, came of age in this decade and led to the party system in its present form. Political clubs (Reform Club for Liberals, Carlton Club for Tories) were also established then, along with basic democratic tools like full, accurate voting lists; in May 1835 Bish was among 200 leading reformer MPs who crowded into the British Coffee House in Cockspur Street, London, to set up a society responsible for 'the full registration of the Liberal Party throughout Great Britain'.

During this period Bish did not confine himself to politics. Shortly before he entered Parliament he was elected master of the Worshipful company of Spectacle-Makers, which he had joined sixteen years before. Few members were from the optical trade. Like so many other livery companies at that time, it was simply a gentleman's dining club whose feasts at the London Tavern traditionally lasted from 6 p.m. until midnight and were a useful opportunity for business and political networking. Or, as the reformer Francis Place alleged of all such City of London events, 'old men, no old women, gossiping, guzzling, drinking, cheating'. Bish succeeded as Master James Harmer, a radical politician and controversial lawyer who not only defended notorious criminals but pursued compensation for Peterloo victims, and was owner of the campaigning *Weekly Dispatch*. This well-read journal advocated reforms many years ahead of its time, such as the abolition of capital punishment, unearthed Establishment scandals and was generally rude about all figures of authority. 'A wax doll' was how it once described the young Queen Victoria. Bish's association with a man many regarded as a revolutionary dedicated to overthrowing the monarchy and church (this perception prevented what should have been his automatic succession from senior alderman to Lord Mayor of London) does not seem to have tainted the newly elected MP. Nor did his opposition to the one reform that the Whig government allowed to sink without trace: making the governance of the City of London less incestuous and more democratic. Except for some individuals like Place, there was no great public pressure to tackle what Place called 'our corrupt, rotting, robbing, infamous Corporation of London'. Livery companies like the spectacle-makers refused to co-operate with the government, subtly undermining its attempts to reform what was at heart an old boys' business club with many members sitting in Parliament. The City of London continued to be a law unto itself.

Otherwise, Bish was a model lawmaker, enthusiastically supporting the reforms which radically overhauled practically everything and laid the foundations of the Victorian Age and Empire and, it could be argued, modern Britain. Unfortunately for him, a character flaw that always tempted him into overstepping the mark reasserted itself and came close to ending his promising political career, and certainly marred it. The bait in this case was prosaic: street improvements in Glasgow. In order to build a major road between Glasgow Cross and Monteith Row, the city council promoted legislation which allowed the disposal of some properties by lot, a perfectly legal and time-honoured scheme. To the embarrassment of the chancellor Althorpe, government law officers did not properly scrutinise the private bill which was passed late in 1831 with wording so ambiguous that it could be interpreted as allowing lotteries to be used to raise money for the streetworks. That was clearly not the intention of Parliament which only five years before had banned all lotteries 'forever'. Bish, Sievewright, Hansard and other unscrupulous ex-lottery contractors seized the opportunity to cash in and exploited the loophole by reinstating the lucky draw specifically for Glasgow. Now firmly back in the advertising game, Bish promoted his schemes by publishing large print adverts throughout the provincial press, all under the cheeky headline 'BY AUTHORITY OF PARLIAMENT'. The familiar red placards reappeared in streets from Regent Street to the Bank of England, puffs were put in national newspapers, lottery offices reopened all over London, and provincial networks of ticket-sellers were reinstated in practically every town, from William Potter, a stationer in Caernafon to Donald Wyllie, a bookseller in Aberdeen. Cooper's Hall was again used as the venue to draw tickets. The three lotteries that were held before the aberration was stopped proved popular despite warnings in the form of jocular ditties in the popular press:

> … ponder, ye who gaze upon
> The tempting Glasgow schemes
> Before your solid cash is gone
> In change for golden dreams

MPs, astonished by the reappearance of an evil they thought they had abolished, made urgent enquiries, traced the unwelcome resurrection to the legislative oversight and soon fingered Bish. Disingenuously, he claimed he was as surprised by Parliament's decision 'as if he had been informed that St. Paul's Church had walked to Tower Hill'. He pointed out he was not a MP when the controversial bill became law, denied he had any hand in drafting the troublesome wording and claimed it was six months from Royal Assent before anyone realised what the wording appeared to allow. His detractors were not convinced. Some accused him of fraud, others spoke of 'State swindling'. The Commons Chamber was packed when an enemy, the Tory Sir Robert Inglis and stout defender of the Corn Laws, moved for the setting up of a parliamentary committee of inquiry and observed, glaring at Bish, that he did not anticipate 'any opposition from more than one member'. Sir

Robert Peel, soon to be prime minister in a minority Tory government, denounced the incident as a 'public scandal' and demanded that those responsible for the fraud be prosecuted. (He later forgave Bish and became his parliamentary 'pair' on occasion.) The beleaguered MP for Leominster unsuccessfully tried to pack the committee with his political allies, claiming that the members proposed knew as much about lotteries 'as Julius Caesar'. (The committee had a wide-ranging remit to investigate all illegal lotteries.) He made a logical case for using state-sponsored draws to raise money for good causes, citing America where they were used, he said, to build chapels, found seminaries, drain swamps and build roads. And he cited the former United States president, Thomas Jefferson, a great supporter of lotteries. Although Bish was eventually cleared of any wrongdoing, parliament had to pass a special law banning further Glasgow lotteries and many MPs were never wholly trusted again. This was a pity, for their suspicion of his motives seriously undermined his visionary proposals to alleviate the plight of a despised and neglected part of the kingdom where, over the coming years, millions of people were to starve to death: Ireland.

Given the boot

CHAPTER ELEVEN

The Odd Couple

When as a young man Bish made frequent trips to Dublin in the late 1790s to help his father with profitable Irish Lottery schemes, he found it 'gay and lively'. It was a prosperous and cultured capital, second city of Britain's empire. Fine coaches, made by local craftsmen from a specialist 2,000-strong workforce, sped along beautifully proportioned Georgian terraces and squares which in their pleasing symmetry rivalled those of St. Petersburg. Rich peers built magnificent mansions and country gentleman fashionable town houses in counterpoint to wonderful public buildings like the Royal Exchange and the Linen Hall. Luxury industries abounded providing a wide range of products and services for the aristocracy and growing middle-classes, such as decorative plasterwork, domestic silver, and gorgeous glass bowls; fine china was not produced locally, but Josiah Wedgwood built showrooms on College Green. The flourishing linen trade, which accounted for more than seventy percent of Irish exports by 1800, lay at the heart of this prosperity. Dublin's economy was fuelled, however, by another source: the 500-year-old Irish parliament. Hundreds of peers and Members of Parliament and their many servants spent millions of pounds each year during the sittings of this ancient body, the money percolating to tradesmen and shopkeepers. Parliament was also the focal point of the social season which took place in winter, with operas twice a week, plays, masked balls, concerts and elegant dinner parties. No wonder young Bish was entranced.

Returning to the city after thirty years he was shocked to find it 'in a most desperate, most deplorable, most disgusting state'. Dublin, looked, he said, 'as if cholera had taken possession of it'. The gravel paths of St. Stephen's Green and other once fashionable walks were choked with weeds. New factories by the Liffey River made for a squalid approach to the centre. Pollution, which caused typhus, was widespread due to inadequate sewers which often became overwhelmed by tidal waters. Some of the elegant squares had become unsightly slums. Half-naked beggars, their numbers swollen by disbanded soldiers and sailors from the Napoleonic wars, were everywhere and amazed foreign visitors like Prince von Pückler-Muskau, who said he always kept coppers in his pockets to throw among them 'like corn among the fowls'. The change was caused partly by the 1801 Act of Union which joined Ireland to England, Wales and Scotland, abolished the Irish parliament and drastically reduced the status of Dublin, which ceased to be a capital. This led to a long period of financial decline as many legislators sold the mansions where they stayed for most of the year and moved out, taking their entourages and money with them. The general recession which followed the end of the wars with Napoleon in 1815 also hit the economy hard. Outside Dublin, in the rural heartland, the plight of the population was far worse. Millions of tenant farmers and their families faced severe hardship after a decade of falling agricultural prices and land values. Only one in fifty could sign their names, and only one in forty children attended school compared to one in four in America, where so many starving Irish had fled, and compared to one in five in Germany and the Netherlands. Famine, forerunner of the great famine disaster of 1845, struck in 1830 and did not ease for four years.

More than ninety percent of the land was owned by absentee English and Irish landlords who, with some notable exceptions, were little concerned by the desperate conditions on their estates. Some were MPs in the reformed House of Commons, but helping their tenants survive was not high on their agenda. The reverse was true. Contemporary newspaper editorials, describing the Irish in terms similar to that used by Nazi propagandists about the Jews, reveal what many in the English establishment really thought about their stricken near neighbour. 'A dirty dot of dominion' was one savagely racist description sometimes used, while a wish that it should be 'swallowed up by the ocean' remained a familiar refrain. The fact that one in three of the thousands of beggars plaguing London were born in Ireland did not help, provoking Lady Craven to complain in her diary, 'Why the poor of London cannot eat brown bread is beyond me.' Not everyone was so unsympathetic. Livery companies did their best. They set up charities like the Benevolent Society of St. Patrick which won the support of royalty and raised considerable amounts of money at gala feasts. Few MPs, however, were worried about the living conditions of the ordinary people of Ireland and the need to provide them with employment and food. Bish was an exception. He had always liked Ireland and the company of the Irish. For years he had donated generously to their charities, organised fund-raising events and frequently holidayed in Killarney, where he bought a property, and other beauty spots. He took every opportunity to draw attention to the plight of Ireland. 'I have but recently returned from that beautiful but ill-fated Country,' he wrote in a published address to his constituents, 'I was an eye-witness to the misery and wretchedness of the People and wish to see their Wrongs addressed.'

He was also an early supporter of a brilliant Irish Catholic lawyer who became a celebrity after successfully campaigning for one of the greatest reforms ever, the right of Catholics to sit in the British Parliament. This campaigner was the flamboyant Daniel O'Connell, nicknamed 'The Liberator', who entered the reformed 1832 Commons as leader of forty-five Irish members (out of a total of 105 Irish representatives) pledged to procure the repeal of the 1801 Act of Union. Six of the repealers were related to O'Connell, who came from one of the few large Catholic landowning families left in

Daniel O'Connell - "The Liberator"

Ireland. One son, John, was appalled by the hostility to his homeland that he experienced in the Commons when he first entered it, and doubly appalled to find this extended to King William IV. Writing in his memoirs of the King's speech opening the reformed parliament, he says, 'The only part ... which his (William's) infirmities or his inclinations allowed him to deliver with any distinctiveness was that in which he threatened Ireland.'

Although Daniel O'Connell had once shot dead a man in a duel and used violent oratory, he opposed the use of force as a means of righting Catholic wrongs. Bish was always firmly against repeal, but he backed the Irish leader's other parliamentary initiatives to alleviate the plight of those suffering under the boot of the Protestant Ascendancy; Catholic peasants, for example, had to pay, by the way of tithes, for the local Anglican parson as well as their own priest. When Lord Grey's Whig administration fell in November 1834 and was replaced by the anti-Reform Tories under Wellington, Bish was prominent in the campaign for reformers and repealers to sink their differences and unite against a common foe. At a packed meeting in Dublin's Corn Exchange, which he helped advertise widely in the newspapers, he was among those who argued successfully for proper political co-ordination of everyone opposed to 'oligarchy and monopoly in Church and State'. O'Connell was at his theatrical and passionate best there, denouncing Tory journalists as 'squalid, miserable and contemptible scoundrels' and attacking Wellington as 'the chance victor of a battle.' Adroitly, he seized the chance to put aside temporarily the contentious repeal issue by promising, 'the Repeal pledge is to be replaced at the forthcoming election by the Reform pledge'. Other meetings followed and in all large towns throughout Ireland anti-Tory associations were formed pledged to overthrow the Wellington administration. This laid the foundations for O'Connell's formal alliance with the Whigs the following year.

Bish also contributed generously at fund-raising events for Irish charities, usually donating more than O'Connell (who was once roundly hissed and booed for giving only £5 compared to £100 from King William). He publicly lauded him as the sole architect of peace in Ireland, even telling MPs on one occasion, 'he has been called an agitator, but he is the only person who can keep the country quiet'. He helped his Irish friend in practical ways. He was one of the organisers of a gathering at the Crown and Anchor tavern in the Strand which raised £1,400 for the Irish nationalist's election expenses in defending his Dublin seat, although the event was disrupted by O'Connell's deserted son who was violently hustled out. In return, O'Connell tried to help Bish during his parliamentary difficulties over the Glasgow lotteries by proposing (unsuccessfully) Bish place men to serve on the Select Committee set up to enquire into the affair. In 1835 Bish suggested the idea of a lottery to raise money to improve navigation on the River Shannon in Ireland, where trade had increased dramatically due to the arrival of paddle steamers carrying passengers and goods. Naturally this would have made the brokers, including Bish, a considerable amount of money. Other Irish and Whig MPs were persuaded to support this ingenious scheme in July at a well-attended meeting at a Palace Yard coffee house, where O'Connell argued there was no evil in lotteries and caused much mirth with his observation that politicians who condemned them 'would be found beginning their *evenings* at one thirty in the morning in the gambling houses of St. James's'.

A few days later a deputation called on Thomas Spring Rice, Chancellor of the Exchequer in Lord Melbourne's administration. He was an Anglo-Irish aristocrat who had represented his birthplace, Limerick, in Parliament for twelve years until 1832 when he was elected MP for Cambridge, and was widely respected for his detailed knowledge of Irish affairs. With his usual eloquence, and with Bish at his side as technical adviser, O'Connell launched into a long speech outlining the way lucky draws could help not only the Shannon but also many other Irish good causes. He argued eloquently that Ireland urgently needed not only river improvements but railways, canals and roads, and a fund to buy land so that small farms could be let to poor tenants. He offered that if the government allowed a million pounds to be raised by lottery, he would raise a further two million in Ireland. Spring Rice, a meticulous though not inspired administrator, did not dismiss the deputation's radical ideas out of hand. He stressed there could be no question of generally using lotteries to make up shortfalls in government revenue, which must have been tempting, considering he faced a budget deficit during his four years as chancellor. However, he said he thought the specific Shannon proposal was 'so little objectionable' that he would put it to his Ministerial colleagues for consideration, though he warned that he did not believe they would approve it. The chancellor assured the deputation 'no man has the good of Ireland at heart more than me'. While the government did not, as he had predicted, endorse the plan, Spring Rice rushed through legislation that autumn to improve the navigation and drainage along the 240-mile long Shannon. Other transport measures followed including an announcement that a railway would be built between Dublin and Galway in order to link the Irish Sea and Atlantic Ocean. The Tory press poked fun. In a satirical report, *The Age* spoke of a meeting at the 'Exchequer Coffee House' where a licence was sought to raise by way of a lottery one million pounds to buy land in certain countries 'on which shall be located a certain number of poor Catholics'. Bish was quoted as saying, 'My life has been a blank ever since lotteries were done up, and the only prize I have drawn was at Leominster ... I shall be happy to manage the lottery for you; for I flatter myself there are few men who are awake to the Cooper's Hall caper than Tom Bish.' He had faced far worse ridicule.

Shortly after entering Parliament, Bish used his fertile brain to conceive the idea of petitioning King William IV to allow periodic meetings of the court and parliament in Dublin. This, he reckoned, would help to stimulate the economy there, as had been the case thirty years earlier before the Act of Union. He spent months working out the logistics and costs and, when he was convinced the plan was viable, he brought forward a motion in the House of Commons. His speech on Tuesday 10 June 1834 was greeted with merciless mirth. Practically everything he said provoked roars of laughter; MPs even jeered his statement that Ireland was in a degraded and disgusting state. This was at a time when hundreds of thousands of Irish people had starved to death. Undeterred by the unrelenting barracking, Bish ploughed gamely on making his case, which was a good one. He argued that the occasional parliament in Dublin would help create jobs, encourage absentee landlords to return, establish new markets by reintroducing English capital and even encourage an incipient tourist industry in Ireland. The cumulative effect of these developments would reduce the cry for repeal of the Union. He managed a few shots against his tormentors who included a number of absentee Irish landlords. 'They knew nothing of Ireland,' he said, 'save the shortest way to get out of it.' They did not laugh at that. Yet despite his eloquent arguments and the support of a handful of Irish nationalist MPs, his motion was not even voted upon as the House was 'counted out' [did not achieve the necessary quorum of forty members necessary for a division].

Nothing if not dogged, and encouraged by the support of provincial newspapers as diverse as the *Hull Packet*, *Hereford Times* and *Caledonian Mercury*, he persevered and, two months after his humiliation in the Commons, published a forty-eight-page pamphlet called *A Plea for Ireland*. This he sent to the then Chancellor and Leader of the House of Commons, Lord Althorp, a dull and unimaginative gentleman farmer promoted well beyond his abilities and unlikely to respond sympathetically. Public support was needed to strengthen his lobbying hand with government, and he began to market his scheme with an advertisement in the *Morning Chronicle* which stated:

LETTER TO LORD ALTHORP

Just published, price One Shilling, A Plea for Ireland, submitting the Outline of a Proposition for holding the Court and Parliament at occasional Intervals in Dublin. By Thomas Bish Esq MP for Leominster.

London published by J. M. Richardson; J. Cumming, Dublin; and may be had of all Booksellers.

Although written in his customary orotund style, this epistle analyses the economic conditions of Ireland with almost Marxist precision and marshals compelling reasons for a radical change of direction. 'Visionary' is an overworked word, but it is a fair description of *A Plea for Ireland*. Bish acknowledges how difficult it is to overturn 'old views and accustomed modes of thinking' but argues for a fair hearing on the basis that his scheme could 'open a new channel for the operation of English capital'. This was a shrewd pitch to investor self-interest at a time when most Englishmen, including a majority of MPs, were barely aware of, let alone able to understand, the problems facing Ireland. He expands on his arguments in the Commons; absent landlords create unemployment, the middle-class Irish are seduced by the delights of London, what few landlords remain oppose the poor laws and thus help create poverty and famine, priests oppose cost cutting measures to slim down a bloated church establishment, nothing is being done to stimulate trade and manufacturing. Yet his plan, he maintains, does not violate political or religious principles or any sectarian rights. 'It is a neutral positive measure offending neither Whig nor Tory, Catholic nor Protestant.'

A telling point is that the English were governing Ireland 'upon hearsay evidence'. He recalls that on a trip up the Rhine river he had carried out a poll of his fellow English tourists and had been astonished to discover only one in twenty had ever visited their near neighbour. This led him to speculate how creating a motive for living in Ireland would make the country a holiday destination: 'It would in a short time become fashionable to visit the exquisite scenery of the North and the South, the splendid bays that indent the shores on all sides, and those remarkable places where history, legend and poetry have alike consecrated to imperishable fame.' In the romantic picture he paints 'the sublime beauties of Killarney, the Giant's Causeway, the Western

Shore and the county of Wicklow' are a good substitute 'for the waters of Montpelier and the charming retreats of Geneva and the Rhine'. Bish even goes so far as to argue that as Sir Walter Scott made Scotland 'popular' with his novels, a single proclamation convening a parliament in Dublin would do the same for Ireland. In purple prose worthy of any contemporary Irish Tourist Board copywriter, he says that people then 'would find the beauties of Italy and Switzerland reflected in miniature in her diversified mountains and valleys, which painters have studied for their picturesque outlines and intense hues. New Cheltenhams, Margates, and Brightons, mineral springs and romantic retreats, would everywhere invite the attention of the stranger; while for the amusements of the turf, for field-sports, hunting, shooting, and fishing he would find himself surrounded in every direction by temptations…'. Remarkably prescient, for 1834.

He backs his vision with statistics. 1,000 MPs and their families, computed at 4.5 people to a family, 4,500 people in all, would travel to Ireland each parliamentary session 'spreading money along the way'. He estimates the cost of his scheme to be £100,000 'compared to the recent Commons vote of thirty million pounds to buy freedom for West Indian slaves'. Steam-packets and railroads such as the planned railroad to Liverpool from London are also greatly improving transport links, argues the iconoclast in his thoughtful analysis; in future, it will take only twenty hours to reach Dublin from Ireland. Bish, a strange mix of spiv and idealist, undoubtedly saw business opportunities in investing in a revived Ireland, but his passionate determination to save its people from starvation was clearly genuine and based on first-hand experience. Throughout this remarkable tract he keeps coming back to the need to repay 'the ancient debt of justice we owe to a part of the empire, which we have misgoverned for centuries'. He also points out the paradox that was the root of Ireland's plight. This is brilliantly summed up in one passage which reads: 'There is not a more fertile country in the world. Irrigated as it is by refreshing streams, rich as it is in a teeming soil, in inland lakes, secure harbours and a temperate and equal climate.' Yet famine still persists because 'in times of great distress, the very provisions thus sent out of the country were purchased here with English money, collected by charity and reshipped to be bestowed upon the famishing people whose industry originally produced them'.

Using his communications skills, Bish followed up *A Plea for Ireland* with letters in the English and Irish press, all laying stress on a central message that his plan, if implemented, would stifle the increasing cries to repeal the 1801 Act. Then came an opportunity: on 16 October 1834 a fierce fire swept through the Palace of Westminster, destroying both Houses of Parliament. At the time Bish was visiting the Killarney lakes with family and friends but he seized the chance to send an urgent letter to Lord Duncannon, briefly Home Secretary under Melbourne and a friend of O'Connell's, arguing that their destruction 'affords an eligible opportunity' for occasional meetings of the Imperial Parliament in Dublin. He suggested the meetings could be held in the Bank of Ireland's premises on Dublin's College Green, since there was a clause in the Bank's lease that required a surrender of its building, on six month's notice, when required for legislative purposes. He leaked the letter to the press, and continued to try and win over hostile newspapers like the *Dublin Evening Post* which had mocked his 'ludicrous' proposal. 'What *Capital Prizes* the Hotel keepers of Dublin would draw!' it said, 'If indeed he [Bish] put his shoulders to the wheel and procure lotteries for the improvement of Dublin, as the Scotch members have done for Glasgow, the New Street and Canal Projectors might be indebted to him!' Inevitably, without parliamentary support (O'Connell and his henchmen regarded the plan, rightly, as an anti-repeal measure) there was never any realistic chance of King William holding court in Dublin.

"There's more hot air generated
down there than up here"

CHAPTER TWELVE

Six Men in a Balloon

It is unclear whether it was disillusionment with politics, following his bruising experience trying to help Ireland, that decided Bish not to fight Leominster again. Other factors may have influenced his decision to stand down at the 1837 general election. Despite the great Reform Act, the electors of constituencies like Leominster still continued to expect bribes, euphemistically known as 'head money', from prospective parliamentary candidates, and it seems that, deprived of his huge lottery earnings, he was increasingly reluctant to pay. His financial position would not have been improved by the financial panic that July, occasioned by the depression in America where one in three banks had failed. 'The confusion amongst the American traders is immense,' reported Daniel O'Connell after a visit to the Irish National Bank in the City of London when the crisis was at its worst.

The champion of Leominster, mainly because of his friendship with O'Connell and his espousal of Irish reforms, was now, unfairly, perceived by some as a radical dedicated to destroying the establishment. Nor had he endeared himself to his rural constituents by voting for parliamentary motions to repeal the Corn Laws; a typical reaction was the letter to the *Hereford Journal* which denounced him on the grounds that repeal would be 'equally ruinous to the Land Owner and Farmer'. His support for proposals to reform the Church of England further alienated his more conservative followers, who transferred their allegiance to a nonentity called Charles Greenaway, an Independent Whig whose only claim to fame seems to have been his position as deputy-lieutenant of Gloucestershire. (He won Leominster and represented it until 1845.) In his retiring address to the voters Bish complained bitterly of the 'perfidy' of those who deserted him, declaring, 'for the sake of Reform, I have sacrificed much.' In a swipe at Greenaway, he said, 'From him, as yet, you can have but promises – from me you have had deeds.' The *Morning Chronicle* hinted that non-payment of head money may have been the real reason for his decision to step down. 'He has not yet come forward owing to causes which our correspondent fears are less creditable to a portion of the electors than to himself,' it said. His departure was lamented by some; the *Hereford Times* described him as 'one of the best-working, honest-voting, members of the reform majority in the House of Commons'. Probably, though, it was a good moment to bow out. The Melbourne government, having successfully steered through Parliament a momentous series of reforms was, like the equally radical Attlee government in the late 1940s, beginning to lose its drive. The Victorian age had begun and Bish, representative of an earlier freewheeling Regency era, may well have felt his buccaneering style would not easily fit into the new culture. The Perth Races that year symbolised his transition; in the heat for a plate of fifty sovereigns a racehorse called Mr. Bish was reported as being 'far in the rear'.

After he left politics Bish initially dropped out from metropolitan life and even left the Garrick Club, explaining in his letter of resignation, 'I shall be very little in London for many months.' No more would he carouse in its green room with Theodore Hook and other wits. He later channelled his energy into entrepreneurial ventures including developing the railway network that was to transform the face of Britain and the lives of its people. His name appears regularly on the various manifestos of the different companies competing to provide rail links and he is listed as a director of the London, Shoreham and Brighton Railway as early as 1835, when he was still a MP. Gone were the days when a London firm of solicitors could refuse to act for this projected line on the grounds that the stagecoaches would drive the trains from the track 'in a month'. He was also a proprietor of the Gloucester, Ross and Hereford railway company, set up in 1836 with a prospectus that promised, among much else, to transport cattle to London in twelve hours instead of fourteen days. This innovation would have greatly benefitted Leominster farmers. Another company which claimed his time sought to connect railways south and north of the River Thames by building a bridge at Horseferry, halfway between Vauxhall and Westminster. He also lobbied for the abolition of tolls on all London bridges in order to speed up traffic over them at a time when the capital was expanding dramatically. The extent of the problem can be gauged by the fact that more than 1,000 market carts a night passed over Blackfriars bridge to avoid paying tolls on Southwark and Waterloo bridges.

Despite his many commitments the ex-MP still found the time to help his friends Frederick Gye and Richard Hughes, who had remained proprietors of the Vauxhall Pleasure Gardens but were struggling to make it pay. By 1836 the popularity of the fun palace by the Thames was declining and takings were down in the face of competition from other entertainments such as the music halls. Charles Dickens, in his *Sketches by Boz*, described Vauxhall by day as 'a porter-pot without porter, the House of Commons without the Speaker, a gas-lamp without the gas'. To arrest the decline, Gye and Hughes decided to refresh their asset by introducing balloon ascents as a main attraction. They paid Charles Green, who pioneered the use of coal gas in balloons and went on to become one of the world's greatest balloonists, to build a huge balloon as tall as a six-storey building. With thirty-six policemen struggling on its ropes, it made its maiden flight from Vauxhall on 9 September 1836, watched by a huge crowd including celebrities such as the foreign secretary Lord Palmerston and the fashionable dandy Count D'Orsay. The sons of Gye and Hughes, who both worked at the gardens, were on board. Nearly a month later, on 7 November, it took off again with an eccentric crew including Robert Holland, who financed the venture and later became a MP, and the flute player Thomas Monck Mason. This time Green landed the craft near the town of Weilburg in the Duchy of Nassau, covering 480 miles in eighteen hours, the longest flight ever made. It was named the Great Balloon of Nassau and Hood celebrated the feat in an ode:

O say, when Mr. Frederick Gye
Seem'd but a speck – a mote – in
Friendship's eye

Balloon ascents were a huge attraction and began to revive the fortunes of Vauxhall. But this profitable initiative was nearly derailed the following year by a disaster. For months, a slightly deranged art teacher and amateur scientist called Robert Cocking had pestered Gye and Hughes to allow him the use of the balloon to make a descent by a parachute that he had invented. He had seen the French aeronaut André-Jacques Garnerin oscillate widely during his parachute descent on a field near St. Pancras in 1802 and had spent the next thirty-five years developing an improvement. His solution was a Heath Robinson contraption of hollow tin tubes, covered with silk, in the shape of an inverted umbrella from which was suspended a basket for him to sit in. Gye and others tried to persuade him to use ash wood not tin, but he argued this would be too heavy. Michael Faraday, a brilliant young scientist who was to make electricity a practicality, also warned him that the ring of tin was not strong enough and needed to be supported by braces. So sceptical was Green of the parachute's ability to carry Cocking's considerable 170lb weight that he agreed to be pilot only on condition that the sixty-one-year-old obsessive inventor was responsible for releasing it from the balloon. Cocking, determined to be the first Englishman to use a parachute, could not be dissuaded. With grave misgivings, the proprietors drew up a contract whereby they agreed to pay him twenty guineas for each of the first two parachute descents and then thirty shillings per time at Vauxhall or elsewhere in the United Kingdom and Europe 'as often as Messrs Gye and Hughes think proper'.

Cocking himself seemed to have had second thoughts when, watched by an excited crowd of tens of thousands of spectators, he stepped into his basket at 7.30 p.m. on Monday 24 July 1837 on a calm summer evening perfect for ballooning. 'He would have given the whole world, had it been his, to relinquish the undertaking,' wrote the journalist John Richardson, who shook hands with him as he clambered in. '[H]is hand trembled violently, and he for the first time became aware of the peril he was about to encounter. It was too late; his reputation was at stake, and he had not the moral courage to recede.' Cocking knocked back a glass of wine, the cords were loosed, and the balloon sailed upwards as the band of the Surrey Yeomanry played the national anthem. At 5,000 feet, and having travelled for a while, Cocking called up to Green and his co-pilot Edward Spencer fifty feet above, 'I never felt more comfortable or more delighted in my life ... now I think I will leave you.' As soon as he activated the trigger mechanism, the balloon shot up to more than 23,000 feet, releasing gas which blinded and almost suffocated both men. Green recalled, 'The immense machine which suspended us between earth and heaven, whilst it appeared to be forced upwards with terrific violence and rapidity through unknown and untravelled regions, amidst the howlings of a fearful hurricane, rolled about as though revelling in a freedom for which it had long struggled.' With enormous skill, and by throwing out everything portable, they regained control and brought the *Nassau* safely down. Cocking's tin tubes, however, collapsed almost immediately and he plunged to his death in a field near Lee Green in Kent, making history as the country's first aerial casualty. Farm labourers carried his body on a litter to the nearby Tiger's Head public house where the landlord Thomas Seares charged sightseers sixpence a time to view the shattered parachute and an additional sixpence to gawp at the virtually unrecognisable remains of Cocking. Frederick

Gye's son, who had arrived at the scene on horseback, attempted to retrieve the body, only to be rebuffed by Sears, clearly a man of character, who argued, 'I can do as I please in my own house.'

It took a magistrate's order to put an end to this gruesome exhibition, by which time so many parts of the failed contraption had been taken as souvenirs that it could not serve as reliable evidence at the inquest. This was held at the Tiger's Head, lasted five days and resulted in huge press coverage; Faraday and the Astronomer Royal Professor Airey were among the many experts who gave evidence. Lawyers acting for Gye and Hughes feared their clients would be held responsible for the tragedy on the grounds that their contract might be construed as offering a bribe to Cocking, but after only forty-five minutes' deliberation the jury concluded Cocking's death was 'a misfortune of his own making'. The coroner concurred and praised Gye, saying he had acted in a 'honourable and humane' way. Nevertheless, the adverse national publicity had badly tarnished Vauxhall's image. Something had to be done.

Bish, Gye and Hughes agreed the most effective way to restore public confidence was to organise another balloon ascent as soon as possible – with themselves on board. In less than three weeks, on Monday 14 August, a huge crowd of spectators cheered as the great *Nassau* balloon again took off from Vauxhall. Aboard were Bish, Gye, Hughes, a Mr. Pell and the eccentric Captain Frederick Polhill, MP for Bedford who, like Bish, fancied himself as a theatre entrepreneur and had lost money running Drury Lane Theatre. The pilot was Green, who went on to make 500 ascents from the pleasure gardens. They had persuaded a professional balloonist Mrs. Margaret Graham and Green's brother to make simultaneous separate ascents as a gesture of support, the former sailing into the sky from Hoxton and the latter from Paddington. Since there was so little wind, all three balloons could be seen over London for hours. Soon, the *Nassau* was becalmed a mile and a quarter above Chelsea College and stayed there for thirty minutes while the six men in its basket drank champagne and toasted the young Queen Victoria (who had given £50 to Cocking's widow) wishing her, presciently, 'a long and prosperous reign'. Only a month earlier Bish had seen the eighteen-year-old monarch prorogue parliament, an occasion which the Hansard reporter described in his usual staid report as 'though out of the line of duty we may record that her Majesty's youth and sex invested the scene with extraordinary interest'. The former MP for Leominster then proposed a toast to 'the sublunaries'. After that they franked two letters following a light-hearted, probably inebriated, debate on whether the letters should be marked 'London' or 'In Nubibus', the last being a typically quirky suggestion from Bish which the others vetoed.

These antics are described in a letter which subsequently appeared in the *Times* signed 'A BALLOONATIC' (almost certainly composed by Bish given its style and his fondness for writing letters to newspapers). Balloons and entrepreneurs seem to go together like fish and chips. Vividly, he describes what it felt like to be so far above the earth, at a time when aerial travel had scarcely begun. He was 'struck by the dead quiet which so instantaneously succeeded the boisterous delight of the tens and thousands we had left on terra firma. During intervals this almost silence of the grave caused (as my impression was) a curious but by no means unpleasant sensation in my ears, which however soon subsided.' He added 'the effect upon myself was quite electric, being unable without pain to look down from any considerable height, even from the top boxes at the opera to the pit ... although I viewed the distances around without fear, I could not without any pleasure look perpendicularly under us'. Any disquiet he felt must have been quickly dispersed by the continuing jollity. Encouraged by the champagne, Polhill offered, according to Bish's letter, to wage 1,000 guineas to 500 that 'he would swim a mile, drive a mile, run a mile, ride a mile, trundle a hoop a mile and (which I forget) something else a mile – all within an hour.' Wisely, no-one took him up. They would have been aware of his record for issuing challenges of this kind; once, while serving in the 1st King's Dragoon Guards, he famously won a one-hundred-sovereign bet that he could walk fifty miles, drive fifty miles and ride fifty miles in twenty-four hours. The confidence-building flight, however, nearly ended in tragedy.

Bish recalls: 'We passed over Hounslow and reached a beautiful place with a mansion standing in its own grounds.' They were above Osterley Park, the stunning country estate of Lord Jersey, created seventy years earlier by the architect and designer Robert Adam for the Child banking family. It was when they decided to descend there that things began to go wrong. Green, experienced and phlegmatic pilot that he was, found difficulty in steering toward a clear landing space amidst so many large trees looming up at him. His grappling iron, designed to reduce landing shocks, caught hold of a tall elm and perched the monster balloon on top, where it stuck fast. 'I likened our car to a huge bird's nest,' writes Bish, 'our situation was truly ludicrous.' More than 2,000 people gathered around the tree, waving and gawping at the plight of the distinguished company trapped in their beautiful crimson and white craft high above the branches. Taking a calculated risk, Green opened the valves gently and the *Nassau* slowly deflated, dropping in one shapeless mass to the ground, where the relieved aviators were helped out. The landlord of the nearby Rose and Crown public house in Hounslow, who had seen the balloon falling, hired a post-chaise which took the amateur aviators back to Vauxhall by 11 p.m. There they joined Mrs. Graham, who also had had to be rescued after her grapple got caught in a hedge near Kensal Green and, with other friends, celebrated their (just about) successful stunt.

Thereafter, balloons became very popular with the masses. 'We came round by Vauxhall where we saw the great balloon go up,' wrote footman William Tayler in his diary for September 22 1837. 'We had a very good view of it, and it was a very grand sight.' The new attraction boosted profits significantly; the following year on fourteen 'balloon' days Gye and Hughes took £6,446 to only £5,544 on fifty-nine nights when no balloons went up. Ascents became increasingly spectacular, featuring fireworks and musicians, though one insane plan to send up a Bengal tiger in the *Nassau* was sensibly abandoned. Perhaps the risk-taking entrepreneurs had learnt the lesson of Cocking's reckless over-confidence.

Déjà vu?

CHAPTER THIRTEEN

Free the Westminster Two!

On Wednesday 29 January 1840, concerned City men, judges and clerics squeezed into the unheated apartment of the serjeant-at-arms, Sir William Gosset, in the temporary barn-like buildings that had housed MPs since fire destroyed the old medieval parliament five years previously. They had come to visit and offer support to the two sheriffs for London and Middlesex, William Evans and John Wheelton, both now in failing health, who had been imprisoned there by MPs. A dramatic constitutional confrontation between the City of London and Parliament, which would take up weeks of parliamentary debate and involve the monarch, had begun. Among the deputation was Bish, determined to help free his two elderly business colleagues. It was to be his last campaign.

The City of London had long acted as a State within a State. Its ancient impenetrable constitution revolving around the court of common council, the main representative body, gave it licence, at least until the 1832 Reform Act, to behave as it pleased. So many imperious edicts were issued on public policy that it became a kind of unofficial mouthpiece of the people of England, blowing raspberries against the national government. Bribery and corruption was rife within the City Corporation, not only in the election of the Lord Mayor, sheriffs and paid officials, but also in the awarding of a wide range of profitable contracts to business cronies. Even the Grey government, active as it was in modernising many other areas and highly successful in reforming local government, was reluctant to attempt serious reform of the City. As Parliament became increasingly representative, a power struggle was inevitable. This duly came, over the commonplace issue of a bill allegedly owed by Luke and James Hansard, the two brothers responsible for printing parliamentary reports. The dispute escalated into a complex drama between the 'Court' of Parliament and the Middlesex county court, which cast the two sheriffs in the unfortunate role of piggy in the middle.

The row began the year before when John Joseph Stockdale, a louche publisher with a reputation for pornography, decided to challenge the Hansard monopoly. His most notorious book was an account of the exploits of the gold-digging courtesan Harriette Wilson, whose clients included the Prince of Wales and Cabinet Ministers. Before its publication in 1825 he had attempted to blackmail a number of public figures, including the Duke of Wellington whose famous retort 'Publish and be damned!' has been repeated many times since by those in a similar position. Stockdale brought two lawsuits against the Hansard brothers for printing parliamentary reports and then initiated a libel action which said they had accused him of publishing an obscene book called *On Diseases of the Generative System*. This tome was spiced up with sensationalist anatomical plates, and prisoners in Newgate had been found enthusiastically reading it, a fact revealed in a report from the inspector of prisons which Hansard had printed. He claimed damages of £50,000 but lost the case after the brothers pleaded the statement was true. Stockdale again sued, but this time MPs ordered the brothers to plead that they had acted on the orders of the House of Commons and were, therefore, protected by parliamentary privilege. The Middlesex county court rejected this defence, awarding the publisher damages of £600, which sheriffs Evans and Wheelton were expected to collect. Parliament ordered them not to do so. Immediately, Stockdale appealed to the Court of

Queen's Bench for the damages order to be enforced. The judges, headed by the Lord Chief Justice Lord Denham, agreed with him and instructed the sheriffs to try and obtain the money. As a result, two bailiffs William Kemp and the unfortunately named James Crook entered the Hansard office in Whetstone Park, Lincoln Inn's Fields and seized printing presses and paper to the value of £600, advertising the goods for sale by public auction. On 16 December 1839, the evening before the auction, Nicholas Winsford, a Bloomsbury builder, offered £695, which was accepted. There was then a stalemate as the brothers, acting on the authority of Parliament, repeatedly issued legal notices demanding that the money must not be paid to Stockdale but returned to them. The issue went back to Denman and his colleagues who ruled that the sheriffs must indeed pay Stockdale his money. Evans and Wheelton were now caught fast.

On the day of the state opening of Parliament, 16 January 1840, MPs acted decisively to assert their authority. The Leader of the House of Commons, Lord John Russell, opening the debate on what was fast developing into a constitutional crisis, outlined the complex legal actions leading up to the impasse, urging the commitment of Evans and Wheelton if they refused to bow to Parliament's will. The Attorney General, Sir John Campbell, warned MPs, 'We must defend the privileges of the House … if you abandon this privilege you will allow every other privilege you possess to be brought in a similar way under the judgement of another tribunal.' The leader of the opposition, Sir Robert Peel, said, 'This privilege of publication is essential to the House in order to enable it to perform its duties.' A motion summoning the sheriffs to the bar of the House was carried by 286 votes to 167, a majority of 119. Events thereafter moved swiftly.

The next day Stockdale, who had accused MPs of being responsible for 'a tyrannic despotism' was examined by them and, after a long debate, was committed to the serjeant-at-arms for contempt of Parliament and thrown into Newgate. The following Monday another long debate began, with Russell moving that the sheriffs be ordered to pay the contested £695 to Hansard. This continued until the early hours when Gosset, a courteous military man knighted for bravery, brought in the two men, dressed in their scarlet robes of office, to the bar, where they bowed respectfully to the massed ranks of legislators, but said nothing. Silence proved their undoing. It was interpreted as an unwillingness to concur with an order of the Commons. Despite their petition stating they were only trying to comply with the law and thus 'putting into effect the Queen's writ', Russell successfully moved that they were guilty of a breach of privilege and must be committed to the custody of the serjeant-at-arms. There followed a farcical interval of constitutional ping-pong. Gosset received a writ of habeas corpus from the Queen's Bench judges to 'deliver up the bodies' of the sheriffs, prompting the Attorney General to tell MPs 'It was a crisis of great moment; they were struggling for the existence of their privileges, and any false step might involve them in inextricable difficulty.' It was decided to tell the judges that Gosset was acting on the orders of 'the Court of Parliament' by warrant of the Speaker. This resulted in his taking Evans and Wheelton to the Queen's Bench where Denman 'remanded their bodies back to him'. Parliament had won.

On Monday 27 January the sheriffs were incarcerated in Gosset's insalubrious chambers where, according to some press reports, they dined on turtle and turbot in company with their wives. The reality was rather different. Both quickly fell ill in the cold cramped rooms, where Wheelton deteriorated so rapidly that within two weeks MPs had to agree to his release because of 'danger of apoplexy'. The campaign to free them took off rapidly. A deputation, led by the Lord Mayor of London went to Westminster to register concern, a petition was drawn up, begging Queen Victoria to exercise the royal prerogative and order their release, and dozens of other petitions arrived in Parliament from mayors and corporations throughout the country. Every day a deputation of well-wishers visited the prisoners, while thousands of others attended public meetings in places like the Freemason's Tavern in Great Queen Street. For Bish and his City colleagues, it proved easy to drum up support. Evans, in particular, was very popular. He was master of the Distiller's Company, a member of an ancient Carmarthenshire family of landed gentry who used his large fortune to give generously to many charities. He was 'a generous and kind landlord, a friend to the poor, and a warm patron of commerce,' according to a contemporary description.

Parliament soon came under fire. *The Age* accused it of 'a most lamentable want of temper, judgement and prudence', while *John Bull* asked 'How is the importance of Parliament supported by cooping up the sheriffs?' In one of the interminable parliamentary debates Daniel O'Connell, egged on by Bish, warned 'public opinion is very considerably engaged'. His MP son, John, later described the debates, however, as 'the dullest, heaviest and dreariest' of all time. Imaginative tactics were used to grab the attention and support of the wider public. Two weeks after Wheelton's release, on Friday 28 February, Bish and the City Remembrancer, the law officer charged with safeguarding the City's status and rights, visited a lonely and despairing Evans. MPs were still voting to keep him imprisoned despite evidence from a Dr. Chambers that he was suffering from a serious liver complaint. It was probably at this meeting that a decision was taken to employ a bolder approach. For the next day huge placards appeared in front of shops and premises throughout the City of London. All displayed the same three questions and answers:

Q Where is William Evans Esq, the Sheriff?
A In prison
Q By whom was he placed there?
A By the Commons House of Parliament
Q For what reason?
A For obeying the law

The placards were printed in the inimitable style Bish had used for his lottery handbills years before: dramatic, alternate, eye-catching

Tom Bish was ejected twice from the Stock Exchange for
defaulting, in spectacular fashion, on his debts

Interior of the House of Commons before the fire of 1834
© Photos.com

lines of red and black letters which attracted great attention. *The Times* concluded, 'Signs are beginning to show themselves that the now long-protracted imprisonment of Mr. Sheriff Evans is exciting still stronger feelings in the minds of a large mass of the people.' The pressure worked.

Six weeks after locking him up, MPs relented and passed a motion which fudged the breach of privilege issue, but allowed Evans to be released. Two months later Stockdale, who had been languishing in Newgate with his attorney Thomas Burton Howard, was also set free. (In 1843, Howard unsuccessfully sued Gosset for wrongful arrest.) The historic clash was over. Later that year legislation was passed which ensured that never again could criminal or civil proceedings be brought against Hansard for publishing parliamentary proceedings and papers.

"I've found one place where
we haven't advertised yet"

CHAPTER FOURTEEN

The Legacy

In the last two years of his life Bish was less active. He lobbied Sir Robert Peel, who became prime minister in 1841, over a variety of issues affecting London businessmen, including the metropolitan improvements urgently needed by the capital as it rapidly grew to become hub of the British empire. He continued to dabble in railway investments, attended livery company dinners, enjoyed visiting Brighton and other resorts with his family, but otherwise kept a lower profile. He died, aged sixty-three, on 27 December 1842 at the vicarage in the picturesque Nottinghamshire town of Southwell, home of his son-in-law the Rev. Robert Hodgson Fowler and his devoted daughter 'Fanny' (Frances Elizabeth). The newspaper obituaries were mixed, as it had become fashionable to decry the old state lottery as an evil almost worse than the slave trade. All agreed, however, that Tom Bish was one of the most famous people in the land. One obituary claimed the media star was more well-known than Peel. Fifty years later it was as if he had never been. Even John Ashton, the great nineteenth-century historian of the lottery, professed to know nothing of him. Astonishingly, in his definitive though rambling *A History of English Lotteries* published in 1893, he could write, 'He [Bish] was the prominent broker in every lottery from 1799 to the last one in 1826 and that is all we know of him.'

Before this vanishing act, references to Bish continue to crop up in the media. For years his name is used to promote sweepstakes. James Bake, who promoted draws at Epsom, was flattered to be called 'the Bish of Derby and Leger lotteries'. A columnist in the sporting newspaper *The Era,* uses the term 'the great Bish' as a term of abuse as the sweeps, he claims, were 'conducted in a rascally manner'. *The Penny Satirist,* in an item entitled 'Mrs. John Jones's Picnic', features elderly Miss Winks, 'who in the good old days of Mr. Bish, had won a ten thousand pound prize in the lottery, and was now living on the proceeds in a snug comfortable way'. In its humorous columns *Punch* magazine makes jocular references to 'our old friend Bish'. Occasionally he is recalled in articles of the Fifty Years Ago variety, such as the 'Some of an old Man's Recollections of London in His Childhood' item that appeared in a 1874 edition of *Aunt Judy's Magazine.* In this, the anonymous author describes Vauxhall Gardens and the drawing of lottery tickets, 'two bygone events still very fresh in my mind'. In 1880, a peculiar story called 'A Prize in the Lottery', featuring Fanny Bish, appeared in *The Girl's Own Paper.* Its author is the Manchester novelist Isabella Banks, writing under her journalist name of Mrs. G. Linnaeus Banks. Internal contradictions, such as portraying Bish as an MP at the time of the Napoleonic wars, prove this is fiction, although the background details are authentic. The highly sentimental tale, which has a suitably moral tale for its young female readers, concerns a poor old crossing-sweeper called Silas Green. He had chosen for his stand a crossing opposite the West End mansion of Thomas Bish MP, whose lotteries, explains Mrs. Banks, 'were better known than [Thomas] Cook's excursions are now'. In a long brown coat, patched and threadbare, he swept the crossing clean day by day, summer and winter, but gradually became more and more decrepit. One freezing day in midwinter pretty, fifteen-year-old Fanny, apple of her father's eye, saw Silas gnawing at a crust he had taken from a rag in his pocket. She asked the servants to fetch him 'a good dinner of hot meat and vegetables' but they refused on the grounds of loss of social status in doing so. Fanny fed him herself and, on his return to the house that evening, asked her father 'a good-natured man, somewhat open-handed' to adjudicate. According to Mrs. Banks' story, 'he idolized his daughter, fostered her charities, and moreover felt himself bound to support the authority and policy of his prime-ministress'. With the exception of Biddy, the kitchen maid, all the servants resigned rather than serve food to the old man. So an arrangement was made whereby Biddy fed him in the scullery, receiving an extra guinea on her wages and the occasional ribbon. One day he was missing from his post on the crossing and a week later a ragged urchin appeared at mansion with a note from Silas saying he was dying and longed for a last sight of his benefactress. With Biddy and a basket containing jellies and other invalid delicacies, Fanny went to the squalid St. Giles slums where she found him in a stifling attic, '…and a tear fell on the withered hand put out to meet hers'. After he died he was found to be not Silas Green, but a rich gentleman who left a will leaving his fortune to Fanny, 'the only being who had taken true compassion on him in his age and apparent poverty'. (It is never explained why he was acting as a crossing-sweeper.) This narrative twist is hardly original and has resonated down the years; its latest manifestation is Channel 4's reality television show *The Secret Millionaire* where wealthy benefactors go disguised into poor communities to search out who needs their cash help. Mrs. Banks concludes with the moral, 'Here was a prize, for which the only lottery ticket had been spontaneous charity – the outcome of a tender nature. Of all the crowds who paid for Bish's lottery tickets with driblets of coin, not one but was actuated by the hope of enormous gain. The lottery man's daughter cast her bread on the waters with no prospect or thought of gain or reward. Yet such a prize had never been won by any of Bish's many ticketholders.' By the end of the nineteenth century such references to the famous lottery entrepreneur had disappeared. But his legacy endured.

Fears voiced by Charles Lamb that the demise of lotteries would kill off Britain's fledging advertising industry proved to be unfounded. He warned that its practitioners 'will be the first, as they will assuredly be the last, who fully developed the resources of that ingenious art, who cajoled and decoyed the most suspicious and wary reader into a perusal of their advertisements by devices of endless variety and cunning; who baited their lurking schemes with midnight murders, ghost stories, crim-cons, bon-mots, balloons, dreadful catastrophes, and every diversity of joy and sorrow to catch newspaper-gudgeons. Ought not such talents to be encouraged? Verily the abolitionists have much to answer for!' After a fallow period from about 1830 to 1845, when Thomas Hood could lament 'few London shops appear at present to keep poets [copywriters],' the industry began to revive.

So successful was it in promoting books that the historian Thomas Babington Macaulay complained, 'All the pens that were ever employed in magnifying Bish's lucky office, Romanis's fleecy hosiery, Packwood's razor strops and Rowland's Kalydor ... seem to have taken service with the poets and novelists of this generation'. The influence of Tom Bish can be found in many techniques, from direct marketing which took off in 1855 following the introduction of a halfpenny postal rate for circulars, to imaginative outdoor billboarding, such as Thomas Beecham's promotion of his patent medicines at seaside resorts by giving local boatmen free sails with advertisements painted upon them. The railway mania of 1845-46 led to the greatest output of mass promotion ever as prospective railway companies rushed out their prospectuses. (In 1837, the year Bish stood down as a Member of Parliament, nearly fifty million rail journeys were made across Britain. Twenty-five years later the figure was 250 million.) Using extensive newspaper advertising, which cleverly manipulated public expectation, it was easy for the companies to present themselves as foolproof ventures to increasingly prosperous and literate middle class families, though all classes clamoured for shares from dukes to farmhands. So frenzied was the demand in Leeds that police had to be employed in force to keep clear the streets leading to the Stock Exchange. At one time the Charles Barker agency, with the financial support of Rothschild, was advertising fifty new ventures a month at a staggering cost each month of £400,000 (£12 million today). The nearest modern equivalent is Camelot's 1994 expenditure of £40 million to launch Britain's National Lottery. Predictably, as with all bubbles inflated by greed, when it eventually burst, thousands of small investors lost their entire savings.

Technology began producing and packaging consumer goods on an industrial scale, which led inevitably to the marketing of these products nationwide. The Great Exhibition of 1851 at the Crystal Palace in Hyde Park was their showcase. It brought together more than 100,000 objects by nearly 14,000 industrial and corporate exhibitors who produced for visitors attractively designed trade cards, price lists, catalogues, posters with often complex tabular layouts, illustrated broadsheets, copper engravings and coloured lithographs. Aquascutum, famous for its outdoor wear and still trading in London's Regent Street, presented its newly-patented showerproof fabric. James Lyne Hancock's patent vulcanised India rubber tubing 'for gas, water, surgical and chemical purposes' was among a number of other innovations advertised for the first time in colour. There was, as Queen Victoria recorded in her diary, 'every conceivable invention' for the attention of the 30,000 people who crammed into the Exhibition – and all promoted by increasingly sophisticated marketing techniques.

Four years later, in 1855, the abolition of stamp duty on newspapers greatly aided the sale of nationally distributed consumer goods. Cheap mass circulation daily newspapers costing just a penny (later a halfpenny), as well as easily affordable weekly newspapers and magazines, all carried advertisements aimed at the consuming public. Advertising handbills also proliferated, their style firmly based on the old lottery posters. May's Washing Powder, Fitch's Patent Fire Wheels, Fry's Caraccass Cocoa, Dr. Ridge's Patent (Cooked) Food, Florador Food ('suitable for seven ages of men') and many others display the same characteristics of bold, shouty, presentation that was so effective early in the century. From 1851, when the bookseller W. H. Smith grasped a business opportunity on the rapidly expanding rail network, many of these advertising posters started appearing on the walls, platforms and booking offices of stations throughout the country. Well preserved examples of the smaller sizes can be seen at Robert Opie's Museum of Brands, Advertising and Packaging in London's Notting Hill. Strangely, though, insets for Pear's Soap, Lux, Oxo, Bovril and other popular brands did not become a common feature of magazine publishing until 1890 – eighty years after Bish first pioneered insets as separately printed cards or leaflets bound in with the pages of magazines. This technique had been rediscovered.

Pear's Soap was inventive in other ways, however, and much bolder than its competitors Hudson's Soap and Sunlight Soap who often relied on clunky imperial images to sell their products. In 1888 it acquired a portrait of his grandson blowing bubbles by John Everett Millais, the highest paid painter of his day. A bar of Pear's Soap was added to this charming picture of youthful innocence, which was reproduced in elaborate chromolithography to become one of the most famous adverts of all time. Twenty years earlier the company organised what has been thought to be the first celebrity endorsement of a product when Lillie Langtry, actress, courtesan and mistress of the Prince of Wales claimed the soap improved her skin. She was following the example of Bish, whose adverts regularly boasted that well-known people, including royalty and visiting potentates, bought lottery tickets from him (whether they did so or not). Some of his lucky draws were promoted with the words 'By command of the Prince Regent' and, as we have seen, he later persuaded the Prince when he became monarch to light the spectacular firework displays in Vauxhall Gardens. Later in the nineteenth century celebrity endorsement became increasingly common, with actresses such as Sarah Bernhardt agreeing to wear hats on stage from the milliners Louise and Company of fashionable Regent Street. Today the technique is common round the world. Images of famous people using or consuming company products can send sales rocketing. When the Duchess of Cambridge (aka Kate Middleton) was photographed wearing a camel-coloured panelled dress from the

High Street chain Reiss to meet the Obamas, demand for the garment soared so spectacularly that the retailer's website crashed for nearly three hours. Marks and Spencer sold out of its grey polka dot dress after Samantha Cameron was seen wearing one at a Conservative party conference. The success of some branded T-shirts was ensured once it became known that actors like Leonardo Di Caprio liked them. Many public figures have been paid for appearing in television commercials, from the former English footballer Gary Lineker, the public face of Walkers Crisps for ten years, to the former deputy prime minister John Prescott who has promoted car insurance.

It was not only in Britain that Bish's techniques were copied. Marketeers in North America, where Volney B. Palmer opened the country's first ad agency in Philadelphia in 1842, imitated his very persuasive style of copy and comic rhymes. Pre-eminent among the early advertisers was Phineas T. Barnum, founder of Barnum & Bailey's Circus, brilliant self-publicist and showman extraordinary whose dwarf 'General Tom Thumb' so amused Queen Victoria with his antics at Windsor Castle. Barnum launched his career, aged eighteen, by writing advertisements for his lottery business in Bethel, Connecticut. This he had set up in 1826, the year Britain abolished the old state lottery. His lively autobiography, which at one time was selling more copies than the New Testament, is revealing. 'I headed the scheme,' he says 'with glaring capitals, written in my best hand, setting forth that it was for a MAGNIFICENT LOTTERY! 25 DOLLARS FOR ONLY 50 CENTS!!! OVER 550 PRIZES – ONLY 1000 TICKETS!!!' The fledgling entrepreneur boasted, 'The tickets went like wildfire. ... In ten days they were all sold.' Like Bish, he branded his business as 'the lucky office', established a network of agents throughout Connecticut, and ruthlessly used press publicity 'to which, more than any other cause, I am indebted for my success in life,' he claimed. Soon, he was issuing tens of thousands of handbills and circulars, 'with striking prefixes, affixes, staring capitals, marks of wonder, pictures etc', along with 'immense gold signs, and placards in inks and papers of all colours'.

Newspapers teemed with 'unique advertisements' and 'homemade poetry'. He explained, 'Selling so many tickets as I did, a prize must occasionally turn up … these being duly trumpeted'.

So successful were these tactics that the young Barnum not only persuaded millhands, farmers, and factory workers to part with their money, but also clergymen, deacons and even Shakers acting 'on the sly'. Complaining that American businessmen did not appreciate the advantages of advertising thoroughly, he advises, 'Homeopathic doses of advertising will not pay perhaps – it is like half a potion of physic, making the patient sick but effecting nothing. Administer liberally, and the cure will be sure and permanent.' So enthusiastically did they embrace this advice that during the nineteenth century advertising became central to selling the American dream.

Mass advertising was also taken up by their counterparts in Britain where the developing consumer culture reflected a steady transfer of power from the aristocracy to the middle classes. A revolution in living was under way. Nowhere was this better symbolised than in the Liberty store founded by Arthur Lazenby Liberty at 218 Regent Street in 1875. Its fashionable clothes, specially designed carpets, curtains, textiles, dress fabrics, attractive china and artistic furniture appealed greatly to the growing professional class. They were presented in a beguiling aesthetic setting, just as Bish and Gye had so elegantly displayed their teas in a pretty Chinese saloon fifty years earlier. Other retailers promoted their goods by making use of the kind of street theatricals so beloved of the lottery men. The Glasgow grocer Thomas Lipton, who built up 300 stores throughout Britain and created the Lipton tea brand, had monster cheeses hauled through the streets to his shops. Thin men paraded carrying signs announcing 'Going to Liptons', while fat men walked the other way holding signs inscribed 'Coming from Liptons'. The cartoonist Willie Lockhart drew weekly posters for him which were used in newspaper adverts and shop windows. Another highly successful retailer, David Lewis, who opened his first department store in Liverpool in 1856, was also fond of stunts. To celebrate the opening of his Manchester branch in 1880, thousands of balloons were released, each carrying a list of the goods for sale and a request to the finder to tell the store where the balloon had landed. One ended its flight in Italy. Lewis also chartered the steamship, the *Great Eastern,* painted it with advertisements for his products and sailed it up and down the Mersey estuary. Not everyone applauded his promotional exploits. In a ferocious attack on the alleged exploitation of the female machinists who made the entrepreneurial clothier's hosiery, boots, hats and capes, *The Manchester City Lantern* commented, 'gas balloons and showy saloons are only the tinsel that diverts attention from the misery and wretchedness of the slave'. The journal, whose proprietor was subsequently fined £100 for criminal libel, added 'puffing means blowing bubbles that burst'. The American businessman Gordon Selfridge equalled Lewis in ingenuity when he opened his Selfridges department store in London in 1909, attracting one million visitors in the first week. After Louis Blériot became the first aviator to fly the English Channel in a heavier-than-air craft, he immediately bought the primitive plane and displayed it in the store. Selfridge, who claimed to have invented Christmas sales and the eternal phrase 'Only – Shopping Days to Christmas' (in 2011 the store started its Christmas display in July), also used blanket advertising coverage. For the 1909 opening he commissioned thirty-two cartoons from artists and caricaturists who worked for *Punch* and ran 104 full-page advertisements for a week in eighteen national newspapers.

The last half of the nineteenth century saw the emergence of famous brands and classical marketing patterns. In 1855, the Bass Brewery started using its red triangle trademark and Colman's Mustard its bull's head motif. Both are still displayed today. Seven years later, one of the world's bestselling alcoholic drinks, with ten million glasses drunk every day, adopted as its logo the harp, symbol of Ireland since the reign of Henry VIII. Surprisingly, though, it was not until the mid-1920s that Dublin-based Guinness embarked on full-scale advertising campaigns; the classic slogan 'Guinness is Good for You!' appeared in its first UK press advertisement in 1929, produced by S. H. Benson of London. Since then its marketing has been blessed with a touch of genius with, for example, the acclaimed 1999 horses and surfers creation topping a Channel 4 and *Sunday Times* poll for the greatest ever television advert. Probably there was no need for formal campaigns in the early days; so many people were prepared to promote the stout for free. As early as 1794 the *Gentleman's Magazine* published an engraving of a seated porter contentedly supping a pint alongside a big barrel of Guinness above the caption 'Porter – Health, Peace and Prosperity'. A Waterloo war hero, critically wounded in the battle, claimed his recovery was due to the drink's restorative powers. Charles Dickens makes frequent reference to Guinness. And, with the exception of Daniel O'Connell, who had invested in a rival brewery, Irish MPs in the Westminster Parliament blatantly plugged it. 'Whenever a man wants a good article, a refreshing and wholesome drink, he calls for Guinness's Best!' declared the Dublin MP Edward Ruthven in a 1835 parliamentary debate on malt liquor. Two years later the young Disraeli drank a pint during a celebration dinner at the Carlton Club.

Since its origins in the nineteenth century, advertising has grown into a worldwide operation that employs millions, directly and indirectly, and has an annual turnover of around £400 billion. The industry touches practically everyone on the planet. As its techniques become increasingly sophisticated and its targeting of consumers increasingly refined, 'exposés' periodically appear. The most famous is probably Vince Packard's 1957 *The Hidden Persuaders,* a best-selling book that accused admen of manipulating people into buying products they do not need. A recent example is Naomi Klein's *No Logo,* an attack on branded marketing that was first published in 2000 and revised in 2010. A more light-hearted approach came from satirical documentary maker Morgan Spurlock in his 2011 picture *The Greatest Movie Ever Sold.* Hilariously, this entertaining look at the mechanics behind the growing practice of product placement on television and films actually managed to fund itself through product placement. These are the

modern equivalents of Lord Macaulay's magisterial denunciations of
the evils of advertising that appeared in magazines 150 years ago, and
follow a pattern destined to be repeated in the future as – for better
or worse – rapidly developing technology devises ever more ingenious
methods of selling products. In fifty years' time current innovations
such as using the Internet to deliver marketing messages are sure to
look as quaintly primitive as the old broadsides do to us now. Were he
alive today in the era of *Mad Men*, mischievous Tom Bish would surely
permit himself a wry smile at the thought of the communications
delights to come and the ensuing fierce debates of how these exploit
the relentless rise of consumer culture. As a pioneer of mass-marketing
campaigns and to a lesser extent, brand identity, he was there first.

PORTER.

The earliest (unpaid) Guinness advertisement (*Gentleman's Magazine*, 1794). So popular was the stout that people promoted it for free (with thanks to the Guinness Archive, Dublin)

SOURCES

ARCHIVAL MATERIAL

Guildhall Library

Records of the Stock Exchange, London
General Purposes Committee minutes 1801-1826, MS 14600
Trustees and Managers minutes 1801-1826, MS 19297
List of Members of Foreign Markets 1832 1835, MS 19525
Applications for admission to membership 1802-1836, MS 17957
A list of newspapers advertising for the London Irish Relief Committee
    1822, MS 07446
Details of exchequer bills and lotteries approved by the Chancellor of
    the Exchequer for raising finance for government, 1798-1811, MS
    29783
Charles Barker Archive (ledgers, account books, correspondence,
    newsletters), 1822-47), MSS 19973-20067
A Collection of lottery puffs, mostly representing dramatic characters
    issued by Bish, Sivewright, S.R.6.2; A Collection of handbills and
    throwaways mostly relating to State lotteries, S.R.6.2

Museum of London Library

W. Wroth, *The London Pleasure Gardens of the Eighteenth Century* Collection
(1896)

British Library

T. Bish, A collection of handbills and newspaper cuttings relating to lotteries, chiefly issued by T. Bish, lottery contractor, 2 vols, Ref 1887.c.15

T. Bish and J. Burch, *Representation of the Camp on Cox Heath,* (1778), Maps 3065

J. H. Burn, *Historical Collections Relative to Spring Gardens of Charing Cross and to Spring Gardens, Lambeth...since called Vauxhall Gardens,* BL Cup.401k.7

Public Record Office, Kew

PCC Wills: Thomas Bish (Senior) Prob 11/1575, Thomas Bish (Junior) Prob 11/1973

East Kent Archive Centre, Dover

Miscellaneous Bank Correspondence, Cobb Family, 1824, EK U1453/ B3/15/144

Hansard

Parliamentary History of England vols XIV – XVII 1826-1827; vols IX- XXXIX, 1832-1837; vols LI-LIII 1840

Parliamentary Select Committee Report on Bribery at Elections, H.C.547, (1835)

Lottery Office: copy of treasury minute for the reduction of the lottery office and granting allowances to reduced officers, published as a Parliamentary Paper, H.C.252, (20 June 1827)

NEWSPAPERS AND JOURNALS

Annual Register
Belfast Newsletter
Bell's Life in London & Sporting Chronicle
Bell's Court & Fashionable Magazine
Bristol Mercury
Caledonian Mercury
Daily Advertiser
Daily News
Derby Mercury
Dublin Evening Post
Edinburgh Review
Figaro in London
Freeman's Journal (Dublin)
Gentleman's Magazine
Glasgow Herald
Globe
Hampshire Telegraph
Hereford Times
Hull Packet
Ipswich Journal
Jackson's Oxford Journal
John Bull
Journal de Paris
Law Intelligence
Liverpool Mercury
London Chronicle
London Evening Post
London Gazette
Manchester Times
Mercurius Britannicus

Morning Chronicle
Morning Herald
Morning Post
North Wales Chronicle
Observer
Oracle
Public Advertiser
Punch
Scotsman
St. James's Chronicle
Standard
Sun
The Age
The Idler
The London Magazine
The Satirist
The Times
True Briton
Trewman's Exeter Flying Post
Westminster Magazine
Worcester Journal
Worcester Post
World

GENERAL

The Oxford Dictionary of National Biography

BIBLIOGRAPHY

Anon. *Coxheath Camp. A Novel in a Series of Letters by a Lady* (1779)

J. Ashton, *A History of English Lotteries* (1893)

I. Asquith, 'Advertising and the Press in the late Eighteenth and Early Nineteenth Century' (*Historical Journal*, xviii, 1975)

F. Bailey, *The Rights of the Stock Brokers Defended against the Attacks of the City of London* (1807)

D. Barham, *The Life and Remains of Theodore Edward Hook* (1877)

P. T. Barnum, *The Life of P. T. Barnum: Written By Himself* (1855)

T. Bish, *A Plea for Ireland* (1834)

A. M. Broadley and L. Melville (eds.), *Beautiful Lady Craven, the Original Memoirs of Elizabeth Baroness Craven* (1914)

A. S. Brock, *Pyrotechnics: the History and Art of Firework making* (1922)

J. D. Burn, *The Language of the Walls and the Voice from the Shop Window* (1855)

D. Chandler, 'There never was his like, a biography of James White,' *Charles Lamb Society*, bulletin no 128 (Oct 2004) pp. 78-95

M. M. Cloake (ed.), *A Persian at the Court of King George 1809-1810. The Journal of Mirza Abul Hassan Khan* (1988)

D. E. Coke and A. Borg, *Vauxhall Gardens: A History* (2011)

F. Coughan, *The Stranger's London Guide* (1821)

E. G. Crowsley, 'Some lesser lights in the Lamb circle', lecture to Charles Lamb Society (1951), unpublished typescript in Guildhall Library, ref M0010346CL

M. E. Daly, *Social and Economic History of Ireland Since 1800* (1981)

G. Daniel, *The Adventures of Dick Distich*, 3 vols, (1812)

F. G. Dawson, *The First Latin American Debt Crisis: the City of London and the 1822-25 Loan Bubble* (1990)

S. Deacon, *Deacon's Newspaper Handbook and Advertiser's Guide*, 5th edition (1881)

C. Dickens, 'King of the Billstickers', *Household Words*, (22 March 1851)

T. S. Duncombe (ed.), *The Life and Correspondence of Thomas Slingsby Duncombe*, 2 vols, (1868)

P. Egan, *Life in London* (1821)

D. M. Evans, *City Men and City Manners* (1852)

S. Ewen, *Captains of Consciousness: Advertising and the Social Roots of the Consumer Culture* (1976)

W. J .Fitzpatrick, *Correspondence of Daniel O'Connell*, vol 1, (1988)

J. Flanders, *Consuming Passions: Leisure and Pleasure in Victorian London* (2006)

J. Francis, *Chronicles and Characters of the Stock Exchange* (1849)

N. Gash, *Politics in the Age of Peel* (1977)

J. Greig (ed.), *The Farington Diary*, vols 1-8 (1922)

C. Greville, *The Greville Memoirs*, 3 vols, (1874)

C. Gudis, *Buyways: Billboards, Automobiles and the American Landscape* (2004)

W. Hazlitt, *Table-Talk, Essays on Men and Manners* (1824)

C. Herbert, 'Coxheath Camp 1778-1779', *Journal of the Society for Army Historical Research*, 45 (1967) p.p. 129-148

C. Hibbert (ed.), *Captain Gronow: His Reminiscences of Regency and Victorian Life 1810-60* (1991)

G. Hicks, *Fate's Bookie: How the Lottery Shaped the World* (2009)

R. Hollis, *Graphic Design. A Concise History* (2001)

J. Hotten, *A History of Signboards* (1866)

T. Hood, 'The Art of Advertising Made Easy', *The London Magazine*, (February 1825)

L. Hunt, *The Autobiography of Leigh Hunt*, 3 vols, (1850)

D. Hurd, *Robert Peel* (2007)

W. H. Ireland, *Scribbleomania; or the Printer's Devil's Polichronican* (1815)

J. Jackson, *A Treatise on Wood Engraving* (1839)

W. B. Jerrold, *The Life of George Cruikshank*, 2 vols, 1882

R. B. Johnson (ed.), *Recollections of Lamb, Coleridge and Leigh Hunt* (1896)

C. Knight (ed.), *London*, 6 vols, (1841-3)

D. Kynaston, *The City of London*, 4 vols, (1994)

W. J. Linton, *The Masters of Wood Engraving* (1889)

E. Lucas, (ed.), *The Works of Charles and Mary Lamb* (1903-1905)

P. Lynch and J. Vaizey, *Guinness's Brewery in the Irish Economy 1759-1876* (1960)

R. C. Michie, *The London Stock Exchange. A History* (1999)

P. F. Morgan, (ed.), *The Letters of Thomas Hood* (1973)

G.W. Mortimer, *A Manual of Pyrotechny* (1824)

H. C. Mui and L. H. Mui, *Shops and Shopkeeping in Eighteenth-Century England* (1989)

T. R. Nevett, *Advertising in Britain. A History* (1982)

D. Newton, *Trademarked* (2008)

J. O'Connell, *Recollections of a Parliamentary Career 1833-1848*, 2 vols, (1849)

R. L. Patten, *George Cruikshank's Life, Times and Art*, 2 vols, 1992

S. Pendleton, *Our Railways* (1894)

J. R. Planche, *Recollections and Reflections*, 2 vols, (1872)

S. Redgrave, *Dictionary of Artists of the English School* (1878)

J. Richardson, *Recollections, Political, Literary, Dramatic and Miscellaneous of the Last Half Century*, 2 vols, (1856)

H. C. Robinson, *Diary, Reminiscences and Correspondence*, 2 vols, (1872)

L. T. C. Rolt, *The Aeronauts. A History of Ballooning 1783-1903* (1966)

H. Sampson, *A History of Advertising* (1874)

R. Seymour, *Robert Seymour's Humorous Sketches* (1834)

C. Sheldon, *A History of Poster Advertising* (1937)

B. Sibley, *The Book of Guinness Advertising*

G. Smeeton, *Doings in London* (1828)

J. Strachan, *Advertising and Satirical Culture in the Romantic period* (2007)

J. Strachan, 'Man is a Gaming Animal, Lamb. Gambling and Thomas Bish's Last Lottery', *The Charles Lamb Bulletin*, No 109 (2000)

D. Stuart, 'Anecdotes of Public Newspapers,' *Gentleman's Magazine* (July 1838), pp. 24-26

G. F. Townsend, *The Town and Borough of Leominster* (1863)

Rev. Trusler, *London Adviser and Guide* (1790)

M. A. Tungate, *Adland: A Global History of Advertising* (2007)

M. Twyman, (ed.), *The Encyclopaedia of Ephemera* (2000)

E. S. Turner, *The Shocking History of Advertising* (1965)

J. Turner, *Historical Hengler's Circus,* 5 vols, (1989)

H. Vizetelly, *Glances back through Seventy Years,* 2 vols, (1893)

W. Weir, 'Advertisements in London', *London* (vol v, 1843), pp.33-48

W. R. Williams, *The Parliamentary History of the County of Hereford, Brecknock* (1896)

M. Wood, *Radical Satire and Print Culture 1790-1822* (1994)

APPENDIX

Ode to Madame Hengler, Firework-Maker to Vauxhall
by Thomas Hood (1830)

Oh, Mrs. Hengler! – Madame, – I beg pardon:
Starry Enchantress of the Surrey Garden!
Accept an Ode not meant as any scoff –
The Bard were bold indeed of thee to quiz,
Whose squibs are far more popular than his;
Whose works are much more certain to go off.

Great is thy fame, but not a silent fame;
With many a bang the public ear it courts;
And yet thy arrogance we never blame,
But take thy merits from thy own reports,
Thou hast indeed the most indulgent backers,
We make no doubting, misbelieving comments,
Even in thy most bounceable of moments
But lend our ears implicit to thy crackers! –
Strange helps to thy applause too are not missing,
Thy rockets raise thee,
And Serpents praise thee,
As none beside are ever praised – by hissing!

Mistress of Hydropyrics,
Of glittering Pindaries, Sapphics, Lyrics,
Professor of a Fiery Necromancy,
Oddly thou charmest the politer sorts
With midnight sports,
Partaking very much of flash and fancy!

What thoughts had shaken all
In olden time at thy nocturnal revels, –
Each brimstone ball,
They would have deem'd an eyeball of the Devil's!
But now thy flaming Meteors cause no fright;
A modern Hubert to the royal ear,
Might whisper without fear,
"My Lord, they say there were five noons to-night!"
Nor would it raise one superstitious notion
To hear the whole description fairly out: –
"One fixed – which t'other four whirl'd round about
With wond'rous motion.

Such are the very sights
Thou workest, Queen of Fire, on earth heaven,
Between the hours of midnight and eleven,
Turning our English to Arabian Nights,
With blazing mounts, and founts, and scorching dragons,
Blue stars and white,
And blood-red light,
And dazzling wheels fit for Enchanters' wagons
Thrice lucky woman! Doing things that be
With other folks past benefit of parson;
For burning, no Burn's Justice falls on thee,
Altho' night after night the public see
Thy Vauxhall palaces all end in Arson!

Sure thou wast never born
Like old Sir Hugh, with water in thy head,
Nor lectur'd night and morn
Of sparks and flames to have an awful dread,
Allowed by a prophetic dam and sire
To play with fire,
O didst thou never, in those days gone by,
Go carrying about – no schoolboy prouder –
Instead of waxen doll a little Guy;
Or in thy pretty pyrotechnic vein,
Up the parental pigtail lay a train,
To let off all his powder?

Full of the wildlife of thy youth,
Did'st never in plain truth,
Plant whizzing Flowers in thy mother's pots,
Turning the garden into powder plots?
Or give the cook, to fright her,
Thy paper sausages well stuffed with nitre?
Nay, wert thou never guilty, now, of dropping
A lighted cracker by the sister's Dear,
So that she could not hear
The question he was popping?

Go on, Madame! Go on – bright and busy,
While hoax'd Astronomers look up and stare
From tall observatories, dumb and dizzy,
To see a Squib in Cassiopeia's Chair!
A Serpent wriggling into Charles's Wain!
A Roman Candle lighting the Great Bear!
A Rocket tangled in Diana's train,
And Crackers stuck in Berenice's Hair!

There is a King of Fire – Thou shouldst be Queen!
Methinks a good connexion might come from it;
Could'st thou not make him, in the garden scene,
Set out per Rocket and return per Comet;
Then give him a hot treat
Of Pyrotechnicals to sit and sup,
Lord! How the world would throng to see him eat,
He swallowing fire, while thou dost throw it up!

One solitary night – true is the story,
Watching those forms that Fancy will create
Within the bright confusion of the grate,
I saw a dazzling countenance of glory!
Oh Dei gratias!
That fiery facias
Twas thine, Enchantress of the Surrey Grove;
And ever since that night,
In dark and bright,
Thy face is registered within thy stove!

Long may that starry brow enjoy its rays;
May no untimely blow its doom forestall;
But when old age prepares the friendly pall,
When the last spark of all thy sparks decays,
Then die lamented by good people all,
Like Goldsmith's Madame Blaise!

ACKNOWLEDGEMENTS

Thank you to the staff of the British Library, Cambridge University Library, particularly the Rare Books Room, Cambridgeshire Library Service, the Guildhall Library, the National Archives in Kew, west London, and the National Army Museum in Chelsea. Marcus Risdell, archivist of the Garrick Club was also most helpful in unearthing some of Bish's letters and I am grateful to George Pitcher for facilitating his assistance. Thanks, too, to the East Kent Archive Centre and Museum of London Library.

A special thank you to John Putnam for sharing with me the contents of the eighteenth-century writing desk belonging to the Rev. Fowler (son-in-law of Bish) which John inherited from his old friend, Rodney Peak, a descendant.

I am grateful to Eibhlin Roche of the Guinness Archive, Dublin, for permission to reproduce the 1794 *Gentleman's Magazine* Guinness advert. The Thomas Bish portrait miniature appears by kind permission of the Luke Bodalbhai Collection UK, courtesy of Bonhams. I appreciate the effort made by Jennifer Tonkin of Bonhams in tracking down this little gem. The Richard Dighton caricature of Thomas Bish 'A view on Cornhill' appears by kind permission of the National Portrait Gallery, London.

Others who helped in a variety of ways included David Coke, Steve Bell, Alan Sutton, Charles Skinner, my daughter Colette Freeman and her husband Edward, and my son Toby. A special thank you to Tanya Izzard for her eagle eye, and sterling work on compiling the index.

I am particularly grateful to Jim Crawley who originally thought this story was worth telling. As ever, Angela Thirlwell was a source of inspiration and encouragement.

The superb cartoons that introduce each chapter were drawn by my old friend and colleague Simon Groves. I am sure they would have delighted Bish.

Catherine Pope of Victorian Secrets has been a marvellously creative and supportive publisher in this project to resurrect Thomas Bish and restore him to his rightful place in advertising history.

ABOUT GARY HICKS

Gary Hicks is a former political reporter who later 'spun' for global corporations and the UK government, travelling worldwide with prime ministers from Harold Wilson to Margaret Thatcher. His first book, *Fate's Bookie: How the Lottery Shaped the World*, was published in 2009. He lives in London and Cambridge.

" What's the odds ?—while I am floundering here
the gold fish will be gone; and as I always
was a dab at hooking the right Numbers, I
must cast for a Share of the Six £30,000 on
the 18th July, for it is but 'giving a Sprat to
catch a Herring,' as a body may say, and it is
the last chance we shall have in England."

INDEX

Victorian Secrets

The Perfect Man: The Muscular Life and Times of Eugen Sandow, Victorian Strongman by David Waller

Eugen Sandow (1867-1925) was the Victorian Arnold Schwarzenegger – a world-famous celebrity, and possessor of what was then considered to be the most perfect male body. He rose from obscurity in Prussia to become a music-hall sensation in late-Victorian London, going on to great success as a performer in North America and throughout the British Empire.

Written with humour and insight into the popular culture of late-Victorian England, Waller's book argues that Sandow deserves to be resurrected as a significant cultural figure whose life, like that of Oscar Wilde, tells us a great deal about sexuality and celebrity at the *fin de siècle*.

"Hugely entertaining ... Waller skillfully places Sandow within the context of the age." Juliet Nicolson, *The Evening Standard*

"Waller...furnishes a narrative rich in stories reflecting Victorian life." Valerie Grove, *The Times*

"Waller's lively, colourful and fascinating book should help restore interest in an unjustly forgotten icon." Miranda Seymour - *The Daily Telegraph*

ISBN: 978-1-906469-25-2 (also available in Kindle and EPUB editions)

www.victoriansecrets.co.uk

Victorian Secrets

Hope and Glory: A Life of Dame Clara Butt
by Maurice Leonard

"Maurice Leonard has a gift for creating character and embroidering it with the most wonderful anecdotes and perceptions." *Jilly Cooper*

Dame Clara Butt (1872-1936) was one of the most celebrated singers of the Victorian and Edwardian eras, a symbol of the glory of a Britain on whose Empire the sun never set. Standing an Amazonian 6'2" tall, Clara had a glorious contralto voice of such power that when she sang in Dover, Sir Thomas Beecham swore she could be heard in Calais. A friend of the royal family, Clara was made a Dame in recognition of her sterling work during the First World War. Her rousing performances of *Land of Hope and Glory* brought the nation together and raised thousands of pounds for charity.

Filling concert halls throughout the world, Clara was one of the first singers to undertake international tours, visiting Canada, Australia, New Zealand, South Africa, and Japan. She travelled with an entourage of over twenty people who fulfilled her every need. Her demands were many, but Clara never failed to delight her adoring audiences. At the height of her career, Clara was locked in rivalry with the celebrated soprano Nellie Melba, almost ending in a libel case when Clara wrote her memoirs.

In the first biography since her death, Maurice Leonard tells Dame Clara Butt's remarkable story, from humble beginnings in Sussex, to her dazzling apotheosis by an adoring nation. With humour and insight, Leonard reveals the woman behind the cultural icon.

ISBN: 978-1-906469-25-2 (also available in Kindle and EPUB editions)

www.victoriansecrets.co.uk